adu/exp

5oo

D0975108

Also by Sheila Nickerson

NONFICTION:

Disappearance: A Map
Writers in the Public Library

POETRY:

Feast of the Animals: An Alaska Bestiary,
Volumes 1 and 2
On Why the Quiltmaker Became a Dragon

Midnight to the North

The Untold Story
of the Woman
Who Saved
the Polaris Expedition

Sheila Nickerson

Jeremy P. Tarcher/Putnam
a member of Penguin Putnam Inc.
New York

Epigraph on p. xv: Reprinted by permission of the publishers and the Trustees of Amherst College from *The Poems of Emily Dickinson*, Ralph W. Franklin, ed., Cambridge, Mass.: The Belknap Press of Harvard University Press, Copyright © 1998 by the President and Fellows of Harvard College. Copyright © 1951, 1955, 1979 by the President and Fellows of Harvard College.

Photo Illustration Credits: pp. viii, xiv, 46, 47, 81: Davis / pp. 48, 115, 151: Nourse / pp. xx, 16, 27, 39, 53, 71, 123: NARA / p. 11: Scoresby / pp. 14, 17, 162: The Indian & Colonial Research Center / pp. 38, 41, 45, 51, 52, 55, 59, 62, 138 (pencil sketches by Emil Schumann): Naval Historical Foundation

Most Tarcher/Putnam books are available at special quantity discounts for bulk purchases for sales promotions, premiums, fund-raising, and educational needs. Special books or book excerpts also can be created to fit specific needs. For details, write Putnam Special Markets, 375 Hudson Street, New York, NY 10014.

Jeremy P. Tarcher/Putnam
a member of
Penguin Putnam Inc.
375 Hudson Street
New York, NY 10014
www.penguinputnam.com

Copyright © 2002 by Sheila Nickerson
All rights reserved. This book, or parts thereof, may not be reproduced in any form without permission.
Published simultaneously in Canada

Library of Congress Cataloging-in-Publication Data
Nickerson, Sheila B.
Midnight to the North : the untold story of the woman who saved the Polaris Expedition / by Sheila Nickerson.
p.   cm.
ISBN 1-58542-133-2
1. Tookoolito, 1838–1876.   2. United States North Polar Expedition (1871–1873)—History.   3. Inuit women—Biography—Juvenile literature.
4. Arctic regions—Discovery and exploration—Biography—
Juvenile literature.   I. Title.
G585.T66 N53 2002
919.804—dc21   2001046470

Printed in the United States of America
1   3   5   7   9   10   8   6   4   2

This book is printed on acid-free paper. ∞

Book design by Meighan Cavanaugh

Dedicated to
the memory of
Tookoolito
of
Cumberland Sound, Baffin Island
1838-1876
Interpreter, Wayfinder, Friend

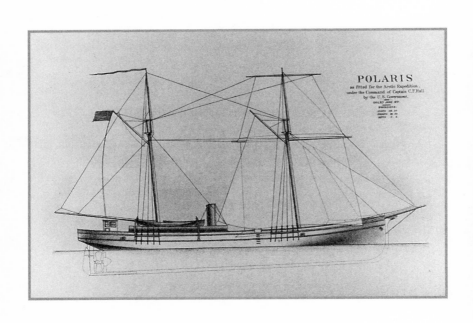

Acknowledgments

Pursuing Tookoolito's story often seemed a solitary journey, but I was never alone. I am humbled by the generosity I met along the way and am deeply appreciative of all the helping hands that reached out:

In Groton, Connecticut, the staff of the public library, especially Barbara Clark-Greene; Carol W. Kimball, historian, who generously shared her knowledge of the area; Lisa Sheley, who took my initial call to the Indian & Colonial Research Center in Old Mystic and who went to work so energetically on my behalf; and Joan Cohn, the director of the Center, who has provided assistance beyond any I might have expected.

In Washington, D.C., the staff of the Smithsonian Institution Archives Center, especially Craig Orr, archivist of the Charles F. Hall Collection; the staff of the National Archives and Records Administration, especially Margery Ciarlante for her knowledge of those papers once collected under the title of the Center for Polar Archives; and the staff of the Naval Research Center, especially Ed Finney.

For readers of early drafts I am grateful: Paul Haskins of Village Books in Bellingham for his valuable insights and comments that made me search deeper; and Pam Finley for her sound judgment.

For computer assistance, without which I would have been lost, I credit my husband, Martin, and Eric Hancock, cyberspace wizard.

I thank Elizabeth Wales, my agent, for her continuing belief, and her assistant, Adrienne Reed, for diligently working her way through the many drafts.

I am indebted to Wendy Hubbert, my editor, for her tireless attention, and her assistant, Allison Sobel, for taking care of so many details.

Martin, my family, and friends have shown great patience, understanding that I had to be absent in many ways. To them, my constant gratitude.

Contents

Chapter Eleven
4:00 P.M., June 5, 1873–Close of Business, December 26, 1873

Chapter Twelve
June 16, 1873–December 31, 1876

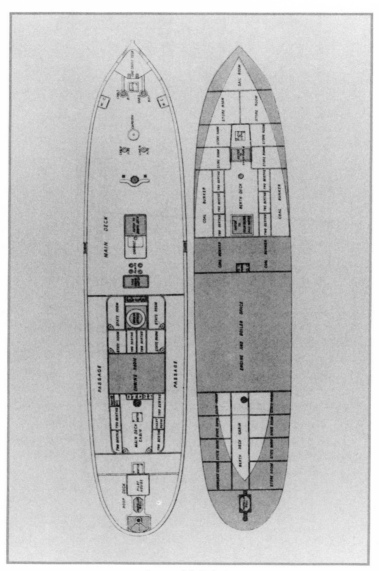

Layout of the Polaris

Behind me—dips Eternity—
Before Me—Immortality—
Myself—the Term between—
Death but the Drift of Eastern Gray,
Dissolving into Dawn away,
Before the West begin—

'Tis Kingdoms—afterward—they say—
In perfect—pauseless Monarchy—
Whose Prince—is Son of None—
Himself—His Dateless Dynasty—
Himself—Himself diversify—
In Duplicate divine—

'Tis Miracle before Me—then—
'Tis Miracle behind—between—
A Crescent in the Sea—
With Midnight to the North of Her—
And Midnight to the South of Her—
And Maelstrom—in the Sky—

Emily Dickinson

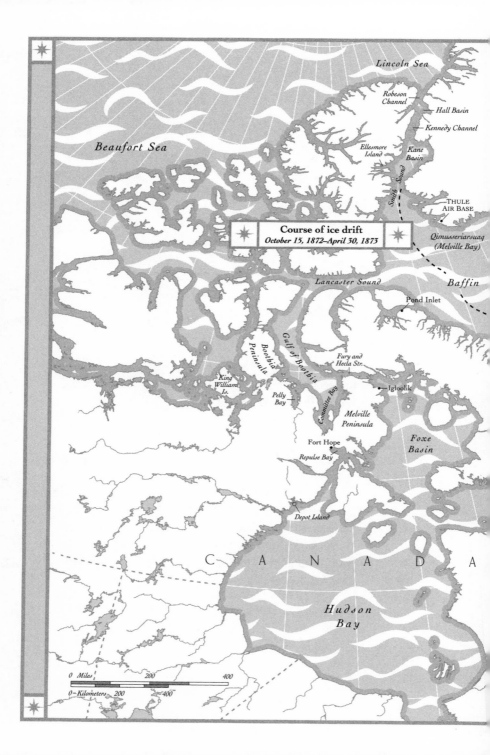

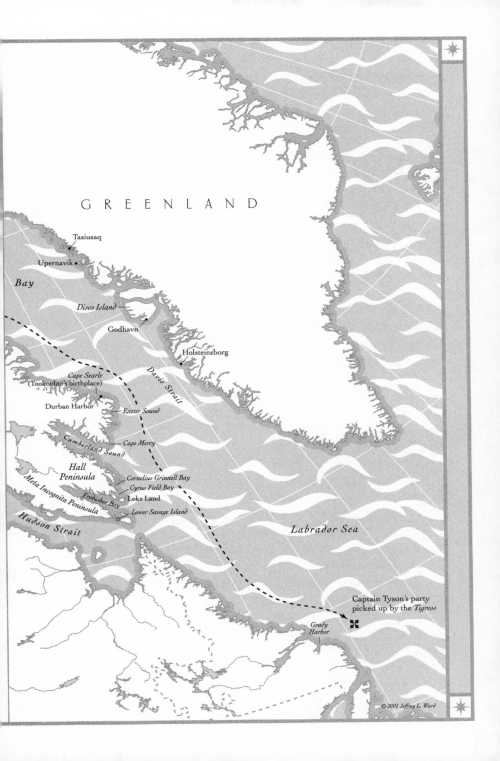

Midnight to the North

Charles Francis Hall with Tookoolito and Ebierbing

Prologue

Perhaps the Arctic intrigues and beckons because, unlike any other place on earth, it has no clear boundaries or definitions. For some, it is the land above the Arctic Circle, an imaginary line at latitude 66°33' north. For others, it is what lies beyond the reach of trees or what is held by permafrost, an identity of temperature. It belongs to no one country but comprises numerous nationalities, languages, and cultures. When viewed from above on a circumpolar map, it appears to circle a bull's-eye center, the North Pole. But that, too, is an imaginary point of wavering location. Mathematical calculations fix a more exact point—the Geographic North Pole. Far to the south and east of that invisible spot hovers the North Magnetic Pole, which has wandered 400 miles since it was first located in 1831. Geophysicists tell us that the North Pole and the South Pole have switched places a number of times. So, too, have cycles of cold moved in and out, refiguring the edges of ice.

Uncertain in physical nature as it is on maps, the Arctic is largely a place of water in motion and transformation (unlike the continent of Antarctica, a landmass). Its central ocean—the Arctic—and the nine seas radiating out from it form a constantly moving and changing wilderness of ice. Human visitors to this land of the midnight sun and the sunless months encounter mysterious phenomena: the aurora borealis, halos to heavenly bodies, mock suns and moons, and the fata morgana. As refraction expands and distorts, icebergs tower, and nonexistent mountains appear to block passage. Mirage invites and destroys, and the eyes are quickly blinded by light—or are kept blind by darkness. Into this frozen land of enchantment full of strange and sometimes terrifying sounds have entered many brave and romantic adventurers. Often they have been driven by flawed motivation and desperate ambitions.

One of these was the American explorer Charles Francis Hall (1821–71). An unlikely candidate for heroism—a former blacksmith's apprentice and self-employed printer with no relevant training—Hall first set his heart on finding survivors of the lost Franklin expedition of 1845–47. When this goal ebbed, he determined to be first to reach the North Pole.

His *Polaris* expedition of 1871–73 failed in this effort and might have gone largely unnoticed except for its drama: Hall died mysteriously, possibly murdered by one of his officers, soon after the expedition got under way; and more than half his party was swept away on an ice floe in one of the most extraordinary adventures of arctic exploration. Present on the ice floe was an equally extraordinary woman: Hall's interpreter, Tookoolito of Cumberland Sound, Baffin Island, known by the whalers as "Hannah." She was the best friend Hall—or perhaps any explorer—ever had.

I first became aware of Tookoolito/Hannah while working on a bibliography of arctic literature of the nineteenth century. While reading Farley Mowat's *Polar Passion* (Volume II of The Top of the World trilogy), I came across excerpts from George E. Tyson's journal of the ill-fated *Polaris* North Pole expedition; there I learned of the remarkable ice drift of nineteen of its members. Certainly, this was one of the most unusual and dramatic tales of arctic endeavor, but, curiously, it seemed largely unknown, with scant reference in the literature. I went to the source cited: *Arctic Experiences: Containing Capt. George E. Tyson's Wonderful Drift on the Ice-Floe, a History of the Polaris Expedition, the Cruise of the Tigress, and Rescue of the Polaris Survivors to Which Is Added a General Arctic Chronology*, edited by E(uphemia) Vale Blake, published in 1874. I was privileged to work with a copy in the Historical Library of the Alaska State Library in Juneau. The book, unsuccessful at the outset and never republished, exists in only a small number of libraries and on microfiche. It is unavailable to the general reading public. Mowat's excerpts provided new access, one that has now expanded with recent interest in the story of the *Polaris*. In his Foreword, Mowat states: "In the late

1950's I set myself the task of shaking the dust from some of them (chronicles of arctic adventure) and of finding a way to restore them to the mainstream of human experience."

What emerged from reading the original account of the "Wonderful Drift on the Ice-Floe" was not only amazement at the physical adventure story—nineteen persons, including five children (one an infant), drift on ice for six and one-half months over a distance of 1,500 miles and all survive—but also questions of the inner story: Who were these people, and how did they manage to live? What went on in their minds and hearts?

The group was strangely polyglot: American, German, Prussian, Russian, Scandinavian, English, African-American, and Inuit. Their forced relationship, born in emergency and raised on necessity, grew in fear and distrust; it ended successfully only because of the loyalty of the two Inuit families involved. Fearing cannibalism—by the recalcitrant European crew members—they could easily have fled, leaving the rest of the party to starve. But they stayed and they hunted. They kept their promise to Hall. One, especially, kept her promise.

Though scarcely mentioned, Tookoolito—an Inuit woman who was the interpreter on board the *Polaris*—emerged as most compelling; her situation and background were unique. Born to an adventurous family well known for its travels, before meeting Hall in Cumberland Sound in 1860, she and her husband Ebierbing (known as "Joe" or "Eskimo Joe") had accompanied an English whaler to England and had been presented at court. She could speak English fluently and could read and write some. She had converted—to some extent—to Christianity. She had traveled for years with Hall on the trail of the lost Franklin expedition and also on the trail of publicity and funds in the United States. She knew the loneliest stretches of the Arctic and the most crowded urban venues of curiosity seekers. She and her family were presented at P. T. Barnum's Museum and exhibited in other settings for Hall's benefit.

Tookoolito respected Hall but would not always obey him. She read his Bible but followed the shaman. She knew well the stories of Jesus but maintained respect for the protective divinity of her people, the goddess who lives under the sea. She both delighted and exasperated him. He often railed at her lapses into what he considered primitive ways, but what successes he achieved he owed to her traditional skills. And after his death, he owed her even more. Hall, perhaps inadvertently, had chosen well the woman who stood weeping at his solitary grave. Neither spouse, lover, relative, nor partner, Tookoolito was yet the closest and most loyal friend he ever had. She was certainly the best qualified to bring his shattered expedition home.

The facts of the *Polaris* ice drift of October 15, 1872, to April 30, 1873, are stated in numerous accounts: in Tyson's journal and the journals of other members of the party, as well as in official U.S. government documents and reports that emerged. But none of these accounts has ever reached a popular readership in modern times. The story of Tookoolito, moreover, is veiled. Hall wrote of her frequently, but after his death other commentators pushed her into the background. Tyson's account of the ice drift, though detailed and riveting, seldom mentions her—and then, only as "Hannah." In the index of his book, she is found in three citations: "Hannah, wife of Ebierbing, 221; learns white manners, 303; afraid of being eaten, 230."

It is easy to be lost in the Arctic, especially if you are a woman, and even more so if you are a young woman or a girl. For many years, as I read casually—and sometimes intently—arctic literature, I picked up on this theme and gradually became obsessed. I wanted to find and bring to the surface women of the Arctic whose extraordinary lives had been ignored, glossed over, historically cast aside—while the men they assisted ran away with the fame. These are the Sacagawea's of the Ice: heroic but forgotten.

Sometimes these women are so faint in the record we get only a glimpse, and all else must remain in the imagination. One such case is "Green Stockings," a young Chipewyan Indian woman who played a role in the overland expedition of John Franklin, 1819–22. The eminent Canadian historian Pierre Berton has called this expedition up the Coppermine River, "probably the most harrowing overland journey in arctic history."

Other cases, closer in time, provide more substance. Captain Bob Bartlett, one of the most accomplished of all arctic sailors and adventurers, credited an Inupiat woman, Kiruk, with saving his life when she rescued his boots from the sinking *Karluk* north of Wrangel Island off the coast of Siberia in 1914.

Ada Blackjack, a seamstress from Nome, was the sole survivor of Vilhjalmur Stefansson's Wrangel Island colony of 1921–23. When all the men of Stefansson's ill-planned and ill-equipped colony disappeared or died, Blackjack was left alone with the expedition cat, Vic, to fend for herself. From

June 22 until August 20 of 1923, she succeeded in doing so. She shot seals and evaded polar bears—her greatest fear. Stefansson, who had organized but not been a member of the colony, wrote prolifically of his explorations and exploits in the Canadian Arctic but never told the story of how Blackjack survived the folly of his Wrangel Island venture.

A story easier to find—and one slightly closer in time—is that of Anarulunguaq. Anarulunguaq was a twenty-eight-year-old Greenland Inuit woman who, with her cousin Miteq, accompanied the Greenlandic-Danish explorer and anthropologist Knud Rasmussen across the whole top of North America in what is known as the Fifth Thule expedition, 1921–24. This expedition—not nearly appreciated enough for what it accomplished—has been likened to Cook's exploration of the Pacific or Lewis and Clark's march across the Rockies. It was an extraordinary feat. Rasmussen, accompanied by Anarulunguaq (whose husband died at the beginning of the trek) and her cousin Miteq, walked and sledged 20,000 miles—from Greenland, to Nome, Alaska—collecting artifacts from and information on a way of life that was rapidly vanishing. What Rasmussen brought us, of the intellectual and spiritual life of the Inuit people, is a gift that cannot be overestimated.

As a young child, Anarulunguaq was about to be killed because she had no father. Among northern peoples, fatherless children, considered a burden to the community, were often killed (and it was nearly always girls who met this fate). Her little brother interceded and saved her life by arguing that she should be spared.

Upon reaching Copenhagen, Anarulunguaq received a medal from the King of Denmark. But her fame faded quickly, and it is difficult today to trace her path—certainly one of the most remarkable of all times.

But here was a courageous woman of the Arctic with a difference: Although equally neglected, Tookoolito had traveled widely outside her remote regions and been recognized in her time both in London and New York. She was buried in Connecticut. There was an unusual trail of documents. There were photographs and letters. Perhaps I could find her and bring her story back from the vaults of ice. Perhaps, through her viewpoint, Captain Tyson's "Wonderful Drift on the Ice-Floe" could take on human dimensions and become something more than adventure. Perhaps, too, it could refocus attention on the significant role of a woman whose story had been minimized.

The history of arctic exploration has been almost entirely that—a man's account, and a European man's account. It has also been a crazed mirror reflecting the personal and national ambitions of those who came for conquest. Here, the chronicle of Tookoolito gives an opportunity for something different: the account of a woman as well as the story behind the story; and how the indigenous people made the white man's adventure possible—and at what price. It can hardly make up for the lack of attention given to the Inuit colleagues of arctic heroes across all times and northern areas, but it can provide a fresh insight. As with the history of Himalayan exploration and the role of the Sherpas, it is past time to bring forth the names and stories of the individual indigenous people who served as essential partners.

The trail to Tookoolito led deeper and further back in time: first, to the government documents related to the *Polaris* expedition (a United States Navy Board of Inquiry followed the debacle); then to the writings of Hall himself. Hall had completed and published a book concerning his first expedition from 1860–62 with Tookoolito and Ebierbing, called *Life with the Esquimaux*, published in 1864. He had left journals from his subsequent expedition from 1864–69 with Tookoolito and Ebierbing; after his death in 1871, these were collected and published by the United States Navy in *Narrative of the Second Arctic Expedition Made by Charles F. Hall, 1864–69*, published in 1879. His journal of the *Polaris* expedition mysteriously disappeared. The Navy published its own account in the *Narrative of the North Polar Expedition, U.S. Ship Polaris*, published in 1876. Hall's 1864 book remains, therefore, his only published personal account—the critical source for determining his attitude toward Tookoolito and Ebierbing. His unpublished journals reveal far more.

Tookoolito and Ebierbing had started traveling with Hall in 1860 and were with him almost constantly until he died in 1871. Between trips with him, they settled among mutual friends in Groton, Connecticut, and established a home there. Soon after the drift on the ice, Tookoolito and her adopted daughter Punny died and were buried in Connecticut, in a small enclosure of Inuit graves.

I followed Tookoolito to Groton and to archives in nearby Old Mystic, which contain letters, photographs, handwritten accounts, and artifacts. She began to emerge. I wanted more than ever to tell her story and commemorate her courage. I wanted to bring her back before she was lost forever—one more set of tracks filled with snow and marbled over by wind. She had led the dogs and pulled the sledges, fished and hunted, cooked and sewed, found food when none was available, kept the lamp burning even after the fuel was spent, made conversation between tribes possible, and helped re-create the story of the lost Franklin expedition. She enlivened kindness in the most desperate situations. Finally, in the blankness of the north where the needle ever spins, she made loyalty her compass and became lodestar of the moving ice.

Arctic history, so dismissive of women and Inuit assistants, is not always fair to white men, either. Charles Francis Hall and his fatally flawed *Polaris* expedition might have remained buried in the obscurity of arctic archives had it not been for the dedicated work of his biographer, Chauncey C. Loomis, who led a small expedition to the explorer's burial site on the northwestern coast of Greenland in 1968. Exhumation and study of tissue samples proved that Hall had indeed died of arsenic poisoning. By whose hand will never be known, though several candidates—all officers of the expedition—clearly qualify. Loomis's work *Weird and Tragic Shores: The Story of Charles Francis Hall, Explorer* (Knopf, 1971; University of Nebraska Press, 1991; Modern Library, 2000) tells a remarkable story of a man so obsessed that death in zealous pursuit of his ambition was inevitable. Loomis's forensic expedition serves as a fitting epilogue to one of the saddest and strangest chapters in the pursuit of the North Pole, a pursuit rife with jealousy, paranoia, and ego run amok. Hall's ill-fated journey—and his lonely grave site on the Greenland coast, "Hall's Rest"—might stand as a monument to the mix of bravery and madness that constituted much of arctic adventure: the high-stakes field of the day. Reflecting current interest in the subject and in Arctic history in general, Loomis's book has recently been republished and is used extensively in new accounts.

Why does the Arctic (as well as the Antarctic) continue to fascinate us? Like so many areas on earth, it is changing, with 40 percent of its pack ice now gone and its tundra melting. It represented, for many years, the ultimate challenge of human being versus nature. It was equivalent to the outer space of our age—the North Pole analogous to the moon. (Recently, a ten-person team searched two sites in Antarctica for microbes. If simple life forms can exist in earth's most hostile climates, it is thought, then also, possibly under the frozen crust of the Jovian moon Europa or on Mars.) Still, it is the realm of speculation.

There is particular interest now in the people and the geographical area of the *Polaris* ice drift story: The area is almost entirely within the bounds of the newly created and vast (770,000 square miles) Inuit province of Nunavut, officially established by Canada on April 1, 1999. The capital, Iqaluit, is indeed at the head of what used to be called Frobisher Bay, close to where Hall, Tookoolito, and Ebierbing began their relationship and travels in 1860. The changing names of this area would alone make a fascinating study: Numerous explorers, starting with Martin Frobisher in 1576, put their nomenclature upon its mostly empty spaces. Those names, meaningless (and often hurtful) to the indigenous inhabitants, have now been replaced with Inuktitut names. "Nunavut," indeed, means "our land." As aboriginal designations are restored, the record of white adventurers—including Hall—fades.

We do not want to lose that record. In spite of all his failings, the nineteenth-century adventurer who dared the Arctic was inherently heroic. He was honored, revered, and often immensely popular at the time. Now, encased in technology, we need to know that such heroes existed. Even if their motivations were flawed, their ambitions selfish, and their cultural views limited, they attempted what we can barely imagine—walking into the ice without protective communications links to a home base and with little knowledge of where they were or what they might encounter. Even up to Hall's time, there was hope of an Open Polar Sea—a concept that had lived on from the time of Pytheas in the fourth century B.C. Sometimes the explorers returned with great accomplishments, sometimes with few; often they did not return at all. Some stayed behind in crude graves, some were committed to the sea through holes cut into the ice, and others were simply swallowed up. But each of their chronicles deserves retelling because they are the stuff of adventure and the substance of physical challenge for which we hunger in a crowded, mechanized world.

Shortly before Hall set out, the November 1855 issue of *Blackwood's Edinburgh Magazine*, from which Chauncey Loomis took the epigraph for his book, put it this way:

> *No; there are no more sunny continents—no more islands of the blest— hidden under the far horizon, tempting the dreamer over the undiscovered sea; nothing but those weird and tragic shores, those cliffs of everlasting ice and mainlands of frozen snow, which have never produced anything to us*

but a late and sad discovery of the depths of human heroism, patience, and bravery, such as imagination could scarcely dream of.

Though the *Polaris* expedition resulted in tragedy and dissension, it was not without its glory. Before his death—and thanks to his Inuit helpers—Hall did succeed in reaching further north (82°11') than anyone to date. The hydrographic, meteorological, and magnetic records he compiled were of use to those who followed (including Robert Peary, who claimed success in 1909), and Hall rightly earned his place in the record book of arctic accomplishment. Above all, he is recognized as the first white man to live with the indigenous people as one of them for long periods of time. He became an expert sledger, setting remarkable records. He proved what numerous others, including the Franklin party, had refused to accept at the cost of their lives: Survival in the Arctic meant living in concert with the Arctic, not in opposition. It was no place for transplanted, let alone dissatisfied, aliens.

Yet Hall was not ready to give in completely to indigenous ways. He appears to have had no sexual interest in the Inuit women, at least none that he would express. A product of his culture, he was both prudish and chivalrous. He was also paternalistic and Protestant. The Inuit in his sphere of influence were his "icy children of the North." He wanted to instruct them in the Bible and imprint them with its moral code. Like many proselytizers of his day—and particularly those in remote areas—he was convinced that he was doing God's work.

In speaking of how Tookoolito had been setting a good example among her people, Hall states: "This shows to me what one person like Tookoolito could accomplish in the way of the introduction of schools and churches among this people. To give this woman an education in the States, and subsequent employment in connection with several of our missionaries, would serve to advance a noble and good work."

At times he speaks with urgency: "Oh that such a noble Christianizing work was begun here (Baffin Island) as is now established in Greenland! What a valuable aid for it could be found in Tookoolito! Will not some society, some people of civilization, see to this matter ere this noble race pass away? . . . It seems to me that the days of the Innuits are numbered. There are very few of them now. Fifty years may find them all passed away, without leaving one to tell that such a people ever lived."

Hall's greatest frustration—and he had many—was that Tookoolito would never quite conform to his image of her or ever quite cross the divide to his side, the country of Christian conduct. Yet he respected and indeed loved her and wanted her to be free of the fetters of superstition and taboo: what he came to recognize as the ultimate imprisonment, the antithesis of his early view of freedom among a nomadic people. He wanted to save her from the terrible fate he kept recording—of the incapacitated woman left alone to die in a sealed igloo.

The cultural fate of a nineteenth-century Baffin Island woman was to be born to a woman alone in a house of ice and to die alone sequestered in a house of ice. It was a situation Hall would not accept but also could not change. At the time of the writing of this book, I was faced with a strangely similar predicament. On the opposite coast, my octogenarian mother was lost in dementia and dying. I could make only occasional visits. Although she was far from deserted in a solitary igloo, she was suffering an aloneness I dreaded but could not change. Tookoolito helped me to explore that aloneness and to find within it understanding and acceptance. She became, in effect, my guide and translator—as she had been for Hall more than a century before. Tracing Tookoolito's travels turned into an expedition of my own— far different on the surface, yet ultimately the same within: discovering what lies beyond the discoverable.

I like to imagine Tookoolito on the day she first set out with Hall by sledge. It was January 10, 1861, a Thursday. The temperature stood at 30°F below zero. Tookoolito, dressed in a new outfit of caribou skins, led the way, tracking for the dogs. She was beginning, in earnest, her extraordinary journey.

I hear her voice—soft and musical, as Hall described it—but cannot quite make out the words. They are the language of water, ordered by a syntax of wind and cold. I strain to listen and to understand. Tookoolito has a story more powerful than time and weather, a story that compels me to chase after her crying, Wait! Tell me more! But she is gone, over the next frozen hillock. She is tracking to the horizon. The dogs are panting and straining behind her. She knows where to set the next camp and how to turn a house of snow into a home snug against storm and heaving sea. She inhabits a landscape of possibility. Everywhere I look, there is ice.

Chapter One

1838–1862

HOW THE WHALES LED TOOKOOLITO AWAY FROM HOME

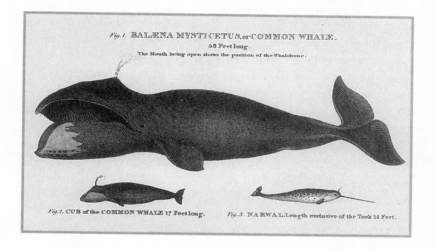

Fig. 1. BALÆNA MYSTICETUS, or COMMON WHALE.
58 Feet long.
The Mouth being open shows the position of the Whalebone.

Fig. 2. CUB of the COMMON WHALE 17 Feet long.   *Fig. 3.* NARWAL. Length exclusive of the Tusk 14 Feet.

If not for the plankton-straining baleen in the mouth of the bowhead whale (*Balaena mysticetus*), we would never have heard of Tookoolito. But during the nineteenth century, "whalebone" crafted from baleen had become a mainstay of women's fashion, and men by the thousands went in bloody search of it. The bowhead, with baleen slabs twelve feet long—opposed to three feet in humpbacks and other baleen whales—had become the most valued species. Its head is so large that a ship's boat, with several men standing upright at work, could enter its mouth for the task of removing the baleen from the upper jaw.

The richest target area for the bowhead became the Davis Strait–Baffin Bay region in the eastern Arctic. From the early 1800s up until the time of the First World War, more than 3,000 whaling ships entered its icy waters, almost exterminating the whale and changing forever the future of the indigenous people, the Inuit.

One of these native people was a woman named Tookoolito who was born at Cape Searle, on the southeast coast of Baffin Island, in 1838. Cape Searle was a whaling station frequented by whalers from both England and America. Only recently had the hunt for bowheads moved over from the east side of Davis Strait (Greenland) to the lesser known west side (Baffin Island). The east side was close to fished out, and new grounds were needed. The opposite side, however, was for the most part unmapped and its topography both dramatic and dangerous, its ice more fearsome, and its weather worse than on the Greenland side. The average whaler was a wooden ship no more than 150 feet in length with little protection from the icy teeth of the sea. Guides, pilots, and local cartographers for the new area were desperately needed. Often their skill was all that stood between a fragile hull and destruction.

Eenoolooapik, an older brother of Tookoolito, filled the bill. Born at a place called Kingmiksok ("dog skin") on the southeast coast of Baffin Island in 1820, he was living in Durban Harbor, south of Cape Searle, when he made up his mind to join a whaler headed to Great Britain. In 1839, he traveled with Captain William Penny of the *Neptune* to Aberdeen, Scotland. There he spent a winter season experiencing a very different way of life—he even attended balls celebrating the marriage of Queen Victoria. But he also became desperately ill. Penny nursed him back to health and returned him to Baffin Island in the spring of 1840.

What the ambitious Penny wanted—and got—from the young, intelligent native of Baffin Island was a detailed map of the body of water named Tenudiackbeek, which was renamed Cumberland Sound. Discovered by John Davis in 1585, it had not recently been visited by white men for fear of the pack ice that lay in front of it. It was rumored to be full of whales, and Penny was determined to have them. Penny tried but failed to get a land grant encompassing all of the sound. Many whalers opposed his petition, as Cumberland Sound had become a desired location. It had also become an increasingly busy crossroads: a significant intersection between the white man's fishery and the indigenous way of life. The Inuit of the area began to settle down, abandoning their traditional migratory hunting cycles and becoming dependent on the goods and foodstuffs arriving by ship. It was a fatal dependence. During the whaling years, the population dropped from 1,000 to 350.

The surgeon on board the *Bon Accord*, the ship that returned Eenoo-looapik to Baffin Island, was Alexander McDonald. He wrote an account of the visitor's winter season abroad. Five years after Eenoolooapik's return, in 1845, McDonald sailed on Sir John Franklin's expedition to seek the Northwest Passage. He and the expedition never returned. The search for Franklin's two ships—the *Terror* and the *Erebus*—and their 129 men would consume decades of effort and expenditure and more than 50 expeditions. Attention in Great Britain, and to a lesser extent in the United States, was riveted on the search until the Crimean War and the American Civil War deflected interest.

The tragedy and the romance of the lost Franklin expedition, heightened by the tireless efforts of the leader's indomitable widow, Lady Jane Franklin, gave energy to the greatest search ever undertaken: the symbol of all that is mysterious and challenging in the Arctic. Both catalyst and black hole, the search caused great stretches of the unknown to be mapped; it also drew into its dark orbit generations of the brave and the dream-driven. One of the first searchers was Captain Penny, who joined the effort during a whaling voyage in 1847 and again in 1849. In 1850, he put the distractions of whaling aside and took command of two Admiralty search vessels, the *Lady Franklin* and the *Sophia*.

When Eenoolooapik, Captain Penny's great hope for dominance of Cumberland Sound, returned home in 1840, his mother and family came down from Cape Searle to meet him. One of his siblings was his very young sister Tookoolito. She was, at the time, undoubtedly in her mother's hood (where Inuit babies traveled naked) and unaware of the significance of her brother's voyage. As she grew older, the whalers called her Hannah. One of the first to meet and make note of her was Sydney O. Budington from the whaling town of Groton, Connecticut.

It was the fall of 1851. Captain Quayle of the *McLellan* out of New London, the sister whaling town of Groton, had left a group of twelve volunteers to overwinter in huts on the shores of Cumberland Sound. It was an experiment to see if a two-season voyage to the area might be worthwhile; in the spring, it was said, whales were in abundance. Twenty-eight-year-old Mate Budington was the leader of this volunteer crew. He met Hannah on the island of Kingmiksok, when she was about thirteen years old. He also met the man who would later become her husband—Ebierbing, whom the whalers called Joe. Ebierbing was the son of Ooyung and Nookerpierung. Nookerpierung's mother, Ookijoxy Ninoo, lived to be over 100 years old; she became a principal source of information for Hall on the history of Frobisher Bay and appears frequently in Hall's accounts of his early explorations. She was one of the many women on whom he depended for information, mapping, and guiding skills and one for whom he held special respect.

Captain Quayle's experiment became an adventure all around. After sailing away from Cumberland Sound to the north, his ship, the *McLellan*, was wrecked in the ice of Melville Bay. Having put his crew on various whalers, Quayle returned to his colony twelve months later. The ship he came on was the *Truelove*, a ninety-year-old bark that had served as a privateer in the American Revolution and was one of the longest-lived whalers in the trade. She was weighted with stories of irony, coincidence, tragedy, and drama—a fitting rescue vessel.

Another member of Budington's party wintering in the sound who was to

Joseph Ebierbing

play a vital role in Tookoolito's life was George E. Tyson. A novice, the twenty-one-year-old seaman kept a written account of the experience. The youthful Tyson, just starting out on what would become a life of extraordinary adventure at sea, was a dedicated journal-keeper whose words would later greatly help to make Tookoolito's story known.

In the summer of 1853, a competitor of Penny's, John Bowlby of Hull, England, sent three schooners to the sound to set up a land base; it failed. In the meantime, Penny, back from a season of searching for

Franklin, took two ships into Cumberland Sound for the winter and had great success. The ships were the same *Lady Franklin* and *Sophia*, newly purchased from the Admiralty and now fitted out as whalers instead of search vessels.

It was that busy whaling year in Cumberland Sound, 1853, when we next hear of Hannah and Joe. By then they were married, or living together in Inuit fashion (there was no ceremony or outward sign observed; a couple simply took up residence together, and a man often had more than one wife). Bowlby took them back to England with him as his guests. There, in his house, Tookoolito and Ebierbing were married before a large company. They were presented at court to Queen Victoria and Prince Albert. They dined with the royal couple. Queen Victoria commented upon them in her diary:

> . . . *They are my subjects, very curious, & quite different to any of the southern or African tribes, having very flat round faces, with a Mongolian shape of eyes, a fair skin, & jet black hair.* . . .

The couple stayed in England for twenty months, returning to Cumberland Sound in June 1855 aboard Captain Penny's *Lady Franklin*. They came back with polished skills, especially Tookoolito, who had taken up tea and knitting. She could speak English quite well, could read and write, and had taken on the vestiges of Christianity. Now, they were ever more valued— Tookoolito as interpreter and Ebierbing as pilot, guide, and hunter. They would never lack for work in the rich and increasingly crowded waters that they knew so well and which the white men wanted so badly to dominate.

Captain Penny settled into a regular routine in Cumberland Sound. After overwintering there in 1855–56, he returned for the season of 1857–58, this time bringing with him his wife Margaret and their twelve-year-old son Billie. Margaret kept a journal, which, though intermittent, provides a rare view of this faraway land. Kindly disposed to the inhabitants of Cumberland Sound, Margaret Penny refers to them as the "kind-hearted Esquimaux" and as her "Esquimaux friends." She presided over a busy social season as hostess of the *Lady Franklin*. On January 1, 1858, she wrote of a "splendid dinner, the greatest delicacies being contributed by the natives, consisting of 6 fine large salmon & 2 quarters of deer." Seventy natives attended. Along with her friend Mary, Tookoolito had been called one of the "two belles of Niatoolak." Wearing a faded silk dress, she was gradually replacing her English wardrobe with copies made of skins.

It was Tookoolito's fashions and polite demeanor that first attracted the notice of Charles Francis Hall when he arrived in Cumberland Sound determined to learn the ways of the north and find the missing Franklin party.

The couple first met Hall on November 2, 1860, on board the *George Henry*, the bark that had brought Hall to Cumberland Sound from New London free of charge. Sydney O. Budington, having survived his earlier experience in the sound and having risen through the ranks, was captain.

Hall, a printer from Cincinnati, had been thankful for the ride because he had next to no funds—and no experience, education, or training for the task he had set himself. Born in rural poverty in New Hampshire in 1821 and having served there as a blacksmith's apprentice, he moved as a young man to Cincinnati. There he learned engraving and, not satisfied, went on to journalism and printing. At the time he met Tookoolito and Ebierbing on board the *George Henry* in 1860, Hall had left behind his pregnant wife Mary and his small daughter Anna in Cincinnati. Whether what drove him was God, dissatisfaction, or the desire for adventure and fame, it was a force powerful enough to lift him from the masses of the obscure, uneducated, and unsuccessful to the pinnacle of singular accomplishment. What drove him was elemental, a fire born to challenge ice.

If not for the largesse of Henry Grinnell, a New York philanthropist, however, Hall could not have moved north at all. Henry Grinnell (1799–1874) was a successful merchant and patron of exploration as well as a founder of the American Geographical and Statistical Soci-

Sydney O. Budington

ety. Born in New Bedford, Massa-
chusetts, to a sea captain father, he
grew up with an interest in the sea.
Partner in a profitable shipping firm,
Grinnell retired in 1850 to devote
himself to philanthropic causes. First
among these was arctic exploration.
He was particularly interested in
the fate of the lost Franklin expedition. In 1850, he sponsored a United
States government rescue mission
that sent out two ships, the *Advance*
and the *Rescue*, and in 1853, he sent
a second expedition north, with the
Advance. In 1860, he gave support
to the arctic explorations of Dr.
Isaac I. Hayes. All were failures.

Henry Grinnell

Hall and Grinnell could not have come from more different backgrounds, but they were drawn together by their shared fascination regarding
the mystery of the Franklin expedition. In spite of the passage of more than
a decade and the largest search ever conducted, both were convinced that
there were not only records, but still survivors, to be found in the vicinity of
King William's Land (an island to the west of Boothia Peninsula, which today is called King William Island). Grinnell endorsed Hall's proposal for a
search expedition and provided a custom-made twenty-eight-foot "expedition" boat and enough funds to pull together basic provisions and supplies.
Best of all, the celebrated schooner *Rescue* of his earlier expedition was assigned to the *George Henry* as tender.

Once on board the *George Henry*, Hall must have felt exhilarated. He was
finally in motion toward the place of his dreams. It was a trip of new experiences—sea sickness, storms, whales, the midnight sun—and constant won-
ders, but a trip that was also strangely prophetic.

Hall was particularly struck by the death of a fellow passenger named
Kudlago, an Inuk of Baffin Island whom Captain Budington had brought
home to Groton the previous fall and whom Hall had hoped to make use of
as interpreter and guide. Kudlago was on his way back home when he be-

came sick. Longing for his native land, his last words were: *"Teikko seko? Teikko seko?"*—Do you see ice? Do you see ice? He was buried at sea in what, for Hall, was a dramatic and moving ceremony. He wrote:

> . . . *At a given signal from the captain, who was standing on my right, the man at the helm luffed the ship into the wind and deadened her headway. William Sterry and Robert Smith now stepped to the gangway, and holding firmly the plank on which was the shrouded dead—a short pause, and down sank the mortal part of Kudlago, the noble Esquimaux, into the deep grave—the abyss of the ocean! Oh what a scene! How solemn in its grandeur and its surroundings!*

An hour later, Hall looked back over the watery grave and saw that an iceberg, a "snow-white monument of mountain size, and *of God's own fashioning, was over it!*" Hall's fixation with Kudlago's death and monument would, in retrospect, seem a mysterious foreshadowing.

Toward the end of the journey, the *George Henry* encountered runaway seamen from the whaler *Ansel Gibbs* anchored in Cumberland Sound. These men, whom Captain Budington fed and supplied, and to whom the sympathetic Hall gave some ammunition and caps, were aiming for Labrador but would find themselves instead caught in a web of theft, starvation, cannibalism, and attempted murder—an infamous story of escape gone wrong.

After this eventful crossing, there were more twists. Hall had planned to launch his expedition to King William's Land from Cumberland Sound. But when the *George Henry* anchored at noon on August 8, 1860, it was not in Cumberland Sound but in a bay to the south at latitude 63°20' north. Hall named it Cornelius Grinnell Bay, in honor of Henry Grinnell's son. Then, after ten days, Captain Budington took the ship further south for the winter, to a bay Hall named Cyrus Field, in honor of another backer. There, a fierce storm soon wrecked both his expedition boat and the long honored *Rescue.*

His plans dashed, Hall nonetheless kept a positive view. He was about God's work and this was a temporary setback; another way would be found. He settled down to wait out the winter, determined to learn everything he could about the place and the people who lived there. In his journal, he describes his first meeting with Tookoolito.

November 2d, 1860.—While intently occupied in my cabin, writing, I heard a soft, sweet voice say, "Good morning, sir." The tone in which it was spoken—musical, lively, and varied—instantly told me that a lady of refinement was there greeting me. I was astonished. Could I be dreaming? Was it a mistake? No! I was wide awake, and writing. But, had a thunder-clap sounded on my ear, though it was snowing at the time, I could not have been more surprised than I was at the sound of that voice. I raised my head: a lady was indeed before me, and extending an ungloved hand. . . . I immediately tried to do honor to my unknown visitor. But, on turning her face, who should it be but a lady Esquimaux! Whence, thought I, came this civilization refinement? But, in a moment more, I was made acquainted with my visitor. She was the Tookoolito I had so much desired to see. . . .

As Tookoolito continued speaking, I could not help admiring the exceeding gracefulness and modesty of her demeanor. Simple and gentle in her way, there was a degree of calm intellectual power about her that more and more astonished me. I felt delighted beyond measure, because of the opportunity it gave me for becoming better acquainted with these people through her means, and I hoped to improve it toward the furtherance of the great object I had in view.

After rescue of the Franklin survivors, if there were any, Hall's secondary objective was Christianization of the Inuit. He looked upon Tookoolito not only as a bridge to her people but as the foundation of a missionary effort among them, one based on the Danish model in Greenland. She was, in all respects, the perfect assistant. While her linguistic abilities would further his work, her spiritual openness would move forward the master plan of God. His search for Franklin was the great object, but Tookoolito's soul was the ultimate prize.

The autumn of 1860 was an unusually warm period. The ice had not taken hold, and, as a result, seals were not available and therefore blubber for the *ikkumer*, or lamp, which was the sole source of light and heat in the *tupic* (a tent made of caribou skins) or igloo. The first time Hall had visited Tookoolito and Ebierbing at their home in what he called North Star Village, he had found her knitting socks and making tea in a cozy domestic scene.

But the second time he visited, he found Tookoolito ill and without such comfort. He became more aware of the position of women and their vulnerabilities. Puto, a single woman with a half-white child, never had enough to eat. Hall gave her some trinkets and 100 percussion caps, a valuable trade item. Kokerjabin, the widow of Kudlago, was devastated with the news of her husband's death. Nukertou, dying, was put alone into a death igloo. Hall records with some detail his efforts to help—and even rescue—such women. These efforts become a major theme and a growing fixation. He railed against the abandonment of women but had, in effect, abandoned his own wife and two young children back in Cincinnati. He expressed effusive gratitude for the kindness and gentleness of women, but surely his own distant wife was kind and gentle; certainly she was long suffering. Was he driven by nineteenth-century cultural sentiments of chivalry and Christianity, or was there something more?

Early on, Hall also began to learn that among the Inuit, custom was everything and not to be resisted. Custom was rooted in ontology, and ontology in the maintenance of balance. Balance—that critical tightrope between this world and the next—was achieved and guarded by the *angakok*, or shaman. The angakok could be man or woman, trained or untrained, a person who drew in the powers of heaven and built bridges between the two worlds. The angakok also demanded—or forced—confession. Taboos were made to please the deities. If rules were broken, the transgressor had to confess publicly. Only after public confession could balance be reestablished and famine kept at bay.

Since his arrival, Hall had been living on board the *George Henry* while making short visits ashore to the natives. As the new year and cold weather set in, however, the time came for Hall to leave the comfort of the ship. His work, he had determined, was to explore and map Frobisher Bay, the substitute for King William's Land.

Here began the serious service with Tookoolito and Ebierbing. Hall took them on as his servants, working largely for food, equipment, and supplies of guns and ammunition. Through their example, Hall learned to live like a native. He learned better than any other white man before him and—in spite of the hardships—to enjoy it. This was his great accomplishment and the one for which he deservedly gained fame. He dressed entirely in native clothes, mostly made from caribou skins. He ate almost entirely native food, mostly caribou and seal meat, sometimes whale skin and blubber, walrus, or duck. He became an expert sledger, traveling thousands of miles through the most difficult of frozen terrains. No matter what his frustrations and difficulties, Hall was never defeated by climate or natural conditions—only by what he carried within him, that most dangerous of baggage.

Preparations had been made. Now it was time to start, with sledge and dogs, into the unknown. Hall would begin by venturing back north, to Cornelius Grinnell Bay, to map its mysteries. This would be his learning ground.

The untried explorer, whose whole knowledge of the Arctic was drawn from books, conversations, and ambition, was now making his first foray into the icy land he had determined to conquer. It was a surprisingly representative experience of what was to follow.

Hall spent his first three nights in igloos while crossing the frozen water with his Inuit friends. On the second night, a storm erupted, and the sea ice began to break up beneath the party. Every step became perilous. The snow deepened, food became scarce, and the hungry dogs flailed and had to be helped to haul the sledge around and over jagged pressure ridges while avoiding hidden cracks in the ice. Here were the themes of arctic exploration: Everything that followed would be a variation of this pattern. In the future, trip after trip, month after month, year after year, the bright beginning would soon give way to peril, the wind would start, and the sea would heave beneath them. Plans would give way to gamesmanship with that persistent guest, starvation. Scenery would shift with shape-changing cold. Storylines would lurch from romance to escapade. The composition was a fugue written in notes as frozen and unchangeable as starlight. With endless patience, Hall followed the sacred script.

In the dark of the fourth night, Hall, Tookoolito, Ebierbing, and their traveling companion Koodloo came upon an igloo where they received water to drink—they had had none all day—and the boon of fresh meat when their host returned home with a seal. Their body tissue was in constant danger of frostbite as the temperature was twenty-five degrees below zero. One night Ebierbing and Koodloo, Hall's sleeping partners on the platform, were absent and he was growing cold. He struggled to get his feet warm until he heard Tookoolito lying nearby ask, "Are you cold, Mr. Hall?" When he answered that his feet were almost frozen, Tookoolito moved down to the foot of the bed, took hold of his feet, and pulled them over to her side where she intermingled them with hers.

Hall was fortunate to have such accommodating friends. Frostbite could claim feet quickly and lead to slow and excruciating death by gangrene. After the night Tookoolito warmed his feet, days of privation followed. Too weak to travel, he sent Ebierbing and Koodloo back to the home base of the *George Henry* to collect supplies. After extraordinary hardship, and barely in time, they returned with the supplies—and with a 200-pound seal! Hall describes the feasting that followed:

> The first thing done was to consecrate the seal, the ceremony being to sprinkle water over it, when the stalwart host and his assistant proceeded to separate the "blanket"—that is, the blubber, with the skin—from the solid meat and skeleton of the seal. The body was then opened and the blood scooped out. . . . Next came the liver, which was cut into pieces and distributed all around, myself getting and eating a share. Of course it was eaten raw—for this was a raw-meat feast—its eating being accompanied by taking into the mouth at the same time a small portion of delicate white blubber, which answered the same as butter with bread. . . .

Blood of the seal: This was the Inuit communion. Over and over, in Hall's account, we experience the euphoria of gorging on newly bagged raw seal. No one held back. No one was slighted. Any stranger coming to the igloo would be included in the feasting, and all shares were equal. This was how any community—no matter how small or large, no matter how rich or poor—celebrated and shared life. Seal meat was not a commodity to be measured and saved but an affirmation to be consumed and relished. It was the energy that made life possible. It was also a token of the kindness essential to the Inuit code—the necessary ticket to heaven. In all regards it *was* life.

After forty-three days, Hall's first trek with his Inuit friends was over. He returned to the *George Henry* and a hearty welcome to find cabin life uncomfortably warm. Scurvy and frostbite were taking their toll on board, and a sailor was lost on the ice. In the Inuit settlements, death stalked. Stories of peril—of escape and loss—abounded. Hall refused to become discouraged, however. As soon as practicable, he set forth for Frobisher Bay: that narrow band of water between Meta Incognita Peninsula (named "Goal Unknown" by Queen Elizabeth, and called Kingaite by the Inuit) and Hall Peninsula (named after Christopher Hall, one of Martin Frobisher's captains in the voyage of 1576). There, he made some startling discoveries. First of all, he determined that the English explorer Martin Frobisher had been incorrect. The body of water he explored on his three trips between 1576 and 1578 was not a strait but a bay. Hall mapped the area carefully, providing new and important geographic information. He found many artifacts left by his predecessor almost three hundred years before and returned boxes of these to England.

Most significantly, Hall collected, cross-referenced, and corroborated Inuit oral history on the subject. It turned out to be remarkably true. If his Inuit informers could accurately pass down such history for three hundred years, Hall figured, they could much more easily pass along true stories of the lost Franklin expedition, an event not even two decades old. If only he could get to the people who had seen and interacted with the Franklin men, he could still, he was sure, find survivors. He burned to do it and sought out every possible informant, filling his journals with myriad evidence.

Meanwhile, on September 4, 1861, Tookoolito gave birth to her first child, a son. She named him Tukelikëta and called him "Johny." When Hall got back from another of his searches twenty-four days later, he was delighted to find the baby and called him "Little Butterfly." Tookoolito was equally glad to see her friend. She and Ebierbing had feared him lost. Although she had almost died giving birth, she had made him two pairs of fur undergarments, a pair of sealskin socks, a pair of duckskin socks, and three crocheted table mats. When he protested, she answered, "I cannot do half so much as I ought for one who has been so kind to us."

Tukelikëta became part of the team of Tookoolito, Ebierbing, and Hall. As the expedition's interpreter, Tookoolito had become adept at eliciting reliable testimony: She knew how to keep from leading the person being interviewed. Unbiased answers were critical to Hall. If he could prove the veracity of Inuit oral history, he could shorten the path to Franklin's men. It was only a matter of time, and time was everything.

But by the end of October 1861 disappointment struck again: The

George Henry was imprisoned in the ice of Cyrus Field Bay for another winter! There would be another nine or ten months of scant supplies. The jawbones of three recently captured whales would be sawed, chopped, and split for fuel, one cord of bone equivalent to four cords of live oak. There was also some timber left from a wrecked whaler down the bay. Food stores were carefully analyzed and apportioned. There would now be only two meals a day. The flour, beans, salt junk, and salt pork would have to be supplemented by native food, including "black skin," or whale skin. Hall contributed, from his private expeditionary provisions, nine 100-pound cans of pemmican and one-and-a-half casks of Borden's meat biscuit. Pemmican, a tinned mixture of dried beef and suet, was a dull and tasteless but essential staple of arctic diet. It could be eaten solid or diluted in soup.

To distract from bad food, boredom, and hardship, there were theatricals and musical evenings on board the *George Henry*. Inuit visitors to the ship would sing, dance, and whistle to the accompaniment of a tambourinelike instrument called the *keylowtik*.

During this period, Hall witnessed the death of one of his Inuit friends, Nukertou. This was his first experience of the local tradition of sequestering and abandoning the dying.

It was nineteen degrees below zero the night Nukertou died. As was the custom, her relatives had placed her in an igloo constructed for this purpose. The lamp in her icy tomb was almost out, and Hall himself was close to freezing. But he would not leave her, even when Nukertou's relatives tried to seal the entrance with blocks of ice. At midnight, as he sat by the dying woman, another attempt was made to seal the entrance. "*Turbar! Turbar!*" (Stop! Stop!), he cried out. Silence. The dying woman was getting colder, her lamp dark. For light, Hall had only his lantern, which he had to hold in his hands to keep the oil from freezing. At three, Nukertou died. Hall placed her head upon a pillow of snow, closed her eyes with lumps of snow, and, as he left, sealed the igloo to keep out the always ravenous dogs. And there the body would stay until the igloo melted down upon her and animals devoured her flesh. The community picked up and moved away. They would not be allowed to visit her remains until some months had passed.

In November 1861, two months after the birth of Tookoolito's baby, as custom dictated, the new mother left the tupic where she had been sequestered with him and visited all the other tupics, even the *George Henry*.

She cast away all the clothing she then had on; she would never be allowed to touch any of it again.

Hall was still focused on his efforts to rescue Franklin's survivors. On December 19, 1861, he declared in his diary: "May I live to see the day when I can visit King William's Land and Boothia, and secure the full history, as it *must* exist among the Innuits there, of that expedition!"

But the reality was, the *George Henry* was still stuck in the ice of Cyrus Field Bay and would be for many months. It would be late summer, undoubtedly, before the ship could break free, and maybe not even then. Sometimes, summer did not arrive, or at least not with sufficient warmth to liberate the prisoners of the frozen sea.

Once Hall got free of the ice, he would have to return to the United States and start all over to scrounge funds for the next attempt. He had no idea that the Civil War was under way. Politics—and the concerns of others—held little interest for him. There was only one driving goal: Find and rescue the Franklin survivors!

In the meantime, the ice-locked winter of 1862 brought another opportunity to save an abandoned woman. It was a time of widespread starvation. Men from the *George Henry* who had been sent out into Inuit encampments to live off the land with their hosts now returned to the ship with reports of desperate situations. Some came back almost dead from hunger. Some came back with the story of a woman who had been deserted.

It was February 21 when Hall set out to rescue the wife of "Jim Crow," who reportedly had been left to die. Conditions were so bad that he and Mate Lamb had to turn back. Four days later he tried again. This time, he and Ebierbing struggled through deep snow and temperatures of seventy degrees below zero to the deserted encampment where the woman was thought to be. The igloos were under snow and had to be located with long snow knives. Finally, Hall cut through the dome of the last, while Ebierbing watched from a little distance off. Inside, he found the woman dead.

Hall, obsessed, carefully studied the grave site to determine the particulars of the woman's death—what had been left for her, what was available to her, and exactly how she had been sealed in. The bedding, he notes, was extremely scanty; her wasted body was covered simply with an old sealskin jacket and "the shreds of a tuktoo skin and piece of an old blanket." But her tattooed face was "youthful and fair."

Conditions during the late winter months of 1862 continued harrow-ingly bad. And then, on the first of April, Hall set out with a party of nine on an exploring sledge trip up Frobisher Bay. The journey, which lasted until May 21, was kept alive by seal meat and an occasional walrus. The milk found in the stomach of a young seal was a particular delicacy. Two puppies were born: an important event. Hungry dogs attacked the sledge and the meat it carried: not a rare event. A ravenous dog could swallow a piece of *kow*, or walrus hide and blubber, one-and-a-half inches square by six feet long in seven seconds. Wolves and polar bears also made their appearance. Inuit friends were found along the way—once, they came upon a village of five igloos. News was exchanged. A baby had died. Another child had been murdered by his guardian who had taken him up to the top of a lonely and rocky mountain, had sewn him up in a seal skin, and had thrown him down into a crevasse, where his frozen corpse was later discovered by other Inuit. Yet another woman had been deserted, without food or light, in a death igloo. This time it was Tweeroong, who had shown Hall particular kindness and exhibited great skill in drawing maps.

On August 8, 1862, Captain Budington arrived by boat at Hall's en-campment to announce that the *George Henry* was nearly free of the ice and that all hands were to proceed immediately on board. After the months and years of waiting, all was now in haste. Hall took a boat's crew seven miles down to the north side of the bay to Farrington Cape to bring back Ebier-bing and Tookoolito. In less than an hour the family was packed and, with their seal dog Ratty, were ready to proceed. Tookoolito and Ebierbing's only concern was that they might lose their infant boy while on board the ship. There was a growing list of Inuit travelers who had sickened and died at sea and been committed to a watery grave. "Mr." Hall had become "Father" Hall, however. The couple would follow wherever he asked.

Chapter Two

1862–1869

TRACK AND DISCOVERIES: TRAVELING WITH HALL

Charles Francis Hall

When Tookoolito, Ebierbing, and Tukeliketa boarded the *George Henry* to sail to America to raise funds for Hall's Franklin expedition, their friends and relations came out in skin boats, surrounding the ship. They cried out, *"Terbouetie!"*—the general term for salutation; there is no Inuit word for "farewell." This was the land of constant leave-taking but no goodbyes.

On August 23, 1862, the *George Henry* reached St. John's, Newfoundland. For the first time, Hall heard, with shock, of the Civil War. The war was gaining momentum. September 17, four days after Hall reached New London, proved the bloodiest day in American history. The toll of the Battle of

Antietam was 23,110 soldiers—Union and Confederate—reported killed, wounded, or missing in action.

For Hall, a new chapter began: fund-raising, traveling, lecturing, and proselytizing for the next trip. Tookoolito and Ebierbing went along with Hall as willingly, and with as much commitment, as when sledging through an arctic storm.

"Everything," Hall wrote to Captain Budington, "must be done to protect the health of these people; the assistance which I hope to receive from them on my sledge trip is too important for us to relax our exertions to have them comfortable." The work was hard and tiring and the exhibition rooms hot. The Inuit family, dressed in their furs and with their dog, came dangerously close to a sideshow act—they appeared in P. T. Barnum's American museum in New York for a two-week stint. The line between promotion for positive purposes and exploitation was as thin as young ice. Exploitation or no, Hall did not make the money he expected. His expenses ate up gate receipts.

Finally, on the advice of friends, Hall curtailed the family's engagements; he would present them only at his own lectures, while largesse from Henry Grinnell would help to keep them fed and housed.

These lectures, in the winter of 1862–63, took place in a number of cities including Providence, Norwich, Hartford, New Haven, Hudson, and Elmira. At Elmira, the Inuit family took sick with colds. Late in January, from his quarters on Fourth Street in New York, Hall wrote to Captain Budington in Groton, asking him to "take the Eskimos into your family." He was weary of nursing them while trying to write and promote his next expedition. But matters worsened. The colds had turned into pneumonia.

On February 28, 1863, Tukeliketa, Little Butterfly, died. Tookoolito, consumed by grief, slipped into unconsciousness and delirium, to be roused only for her son's burial in Groton. Her one desire was to join him in death. She was ill enough almost to succeed. Several weeks later, following the tradition of her people, she placed his playthings on his grave. At a subsequent visit, she was distressed to discover one item, a brightly colored tin pail, missing.

In the world of the Civil War, cold and blockades slowed the action. Famine gripped Richmond, and the pressures on Vicksburg intensified.

On July 16, 1863, the *George Henry* was wrecked on one of the Savage Islands in Hudson's Strait, about 100 miles south of where the *Rescue* had been destroyed. After a perilous month of drifting in five small boats, the captain (no longer Budington but Christopher B. Chapell) and crew were all saved.

Was it an omen that the ship that had brought Hall to Baffin Island and carried him back to the United States with Tookoolito, Ebierbing, and Tukeliketa—the ship associated with the name Budington—was now lost in the ice? Hall thought enough of the event to include a New London newspaper account of it in the appendix to his *Life with the Esquimaux . . .* , the account of his first expedition.

In retrospect, the wreck of the *George Henry* represents a deeper wreckage: It came at the time when the Union was torn and bleeding; it was also the time when Hall and Budington crashed on the shoals of jealousy; and the lives of Tookoolito and Ebierbing hung in the balance.

At this time—the summer of 1863—Tookoolito and Ebierbing were with Hall in Nyack, New York. They were living on a farm owned by a Mrs. Quick, assisting with farmwork to offset boarding charges while Hall struggled to complete his book. Financial pressures had become severe, and it was a period of enormous strain.

By November, Hall had moved to New York City to be closer to his editors at Harper Brothers, who had given him an extension on his contract, while his "Esquimaux Children" stayed in Nyack.

Driven by poverty and obsession, Hall was laboring to finish his manuscript and make preparations to return to the Arctic for his second exploration. To assist him with the manuscript, he had hired an English explorer and writer of the minor ranks named William Parker Snow, who had been engaged in the Franklin search. Snow proved as jealous and difficult as any arctic adventurer—and certainly as paranoid as his employer. Apprenticed at age thirteen to a small brig sailing to Calcutta, Snow seemed to have achieved nothing in life but challenge laced with litigation and penury. He had argued with authorities in the Falkland Islands and England before taking up with Hall. The prickly relationship between the two men deteriorated into rancor. Snow sued Hall for back pay and took him to court.

In the meantime, Hall's relationship with Budington had frayed as well. In June 1863, Hall learned from their mutual friend Henry Grinnell that Budington, set to leave on a whaling cruise to Baffin Island in July, had proposed taking Tookoolito and Ebierbing with him, to return them to their home. Hall was furious and heaped invective on his longtime friend and cohort, breaking off communications as Budington sailed away without the Inuit couple to their place of shared memories. Hall was determined to keep his "Esquimaux Children" to himself. His outpost in Nyack might as well have been called Hall's Rage. It was a bitter locus from which he never quite moved; its narrow constraints would shape events to come.

In spite of the break with Sydney Budington, however, communications between Sarah Budington and Hall, Tookoolito, and Ebierbing continued. The captain's wife, a former schoolteacher, had tutored previous visitors from Cumberland Sound and was clearly sympathetic to the situation of Inuit visitors. Tookoolito always referred to Mrs. Budington, an emotional anchor, as "Mother Budington" or "pretty Mother." She wrote to her of Tuke-liketa, and Mrs. Budington reported on visiting the child's grave. Hall wrote: "There are many passages in your letter that bespeak a soul holding communion with Heaven. It gives me great pleasure that I have as devoted friends as the few I have." She passed along news from her husband on the shores of Baffin Island. Ookijoxy Ninoo, Ebierbing's grandmother, had died. The captain was caught in the ice. Hall regretted that Budington had not gone where he had urged him to go, into Hudson Bay and up Roes Welcome Sound to Wager Inlet; there he would have found open water and whales.

The summer and fall of 1863 and the beginning of 1864 was not a good time to be looking for financial assistance for arctic exploration. The Civil War was now raging and casualties mounting. The Battle of Gettysburg, July 1–3, 1863, riveted and shook the East Coast. Vicksburg surrendered the next day. The Battle of Chickamauga followed as well as sieges throughout the south. Philanthropists and men of influence had other matters on their minds.

Lacking funds and support, Hall took what he could get—free passage to Hudson Bay on the whaler *Monticello* out of New London, under Captain Edward A. Chapel. First, however, he had to disentangle himself from Snow. Once the Marine Court in New York threw out Snow's case, Hall was free to leave the country. He and his charges did so almost immediately—on July 1, 1864, the one-year anniversary of the first day of the Battle of Gettysburg. Though liberated, he had been kept by the legal wrangling from a visit to his wife and daughter and son in Cincinnati. He was not to return for five years.

The plan was to get to Repulse Bay—the staging area for Hall's long-planned expedition to Boothia Peninsula and King William's Land. First, the *Monticello* anchored at Depot Island, a popular whaling site at the mouth of Roes Welcome Sound. Hall then arranged to have himself and his party taken by the ship's tender 100 miles north up the coast to Wager Bay. His party consisted of himself, Tookoolito and Ebierbing, and also an assistant whom he hired from one of the neighboring whalers. His outfit was made up of a twenty-eight-foot boat, the *Sylvia*, named for Grinnell's daughter, and 1,400 pounds of supplies.

Mistakenly, the tender captain dropped off the north-bound party forty miles south of the designated place. This error would cost Hall a whole season, thus beginning his second journey of exploration in frustration and delay. The survivors of the Franklin party—who had already waited for seventeen years at least—would have to endure another hungry winter.

Settled at Repulse Bay, Hall lived first in a tupic and later in an igloo, thawing icy ink in order to write his journal each night. An outbreak of boils and abscesses, particularly on his eyelids, and the onset of stormy weather began to crack Hall's optimism. Depression and frustration took their toll as the darkness of winter closed in. Rankled by the superstitions and taboos of his Inuit hosts, Hall found his pleasure in their warm hospitality giving way to lack of respect. In September, visitors lay about Hall's tupic, talking with Tookoolito and Ebierbing, and eating their scant food supply of pemmican, tallow candles, and rotten meat. Increasingly, they enforced taboos. Tookoolito felt compelled by custom to leave the protective warmth of the caribou tent in order to mend her caribou stockings. Tookoolito's health was weakening from following the strict rules. In November, the angakok, Artooa, told Ebierbing, who was suffering from rheumatism, that the two men had to exchange wives for the night. Ebierbing, wanting to be cured, assented, though Tookoolito did not. Hall intervened. With his coaching, Tookoolito dressed for bed in many layers. The angakok was not able to penetrate them. Then, when Hall summoned her at 1:45 in the morning to get his breakfast, she jumped out of bed, and the angakok, defeated, stormed out of the igloo.

Though the angakok would increasingly grate against his Christian sensibilities, Hall let himself be worked on when he was sick that same month. The angakok told him his illness resulted from having eaten *toodnoo* (caribou fat) prepared in a way not according to custom during his previous expedition and from having left behind in his own country an enemy who had tried to do him harm—an enemy bitter enough to kill him and to rejoice at his death. Hall acknowledged both claims. He thought right away of William Parker Snow; but did he think of Budington? Snow was an irritant, but Budington was a danger. He and Hall were now locked in a jealous combat that would prove more deadly than Hall could have imagined.

Hall followed the shaman's prescription—abandoning certain articles of clothing he had been given—and got well. The Inuit were delighted. By the following month, he was out with them on the sea ice hunting walrus and seal.

Tookoolito had prepared him well. She had sewn seven complete sets of fur suits—two for Hall, two for her husband, one for Rudolph, the hired hand, and two for herself. She had also prepared bedding. To accomplish this, she had worked fifteen hours a day for thirty days. Now, as the men hunted out on the ice, Tookoolito kept a beacon light burning on a hilltop.

Back home, General Sherman was completing his march to the sea and laying siege to Savannah until he could offer the city to President Lincoln. In the Indian Ocean, the Confederate steamship *Shenandoah* ended the year by capturing and destroying the unarmed bark *Delphine*.

At Hall's encampment, New Year's Day 1865 was celebrated with a breakfast of frozen venison and toodnoo, followed by a 2:00 P.M. feast of vegetable and pemmican soup and sea bread, with coffee, isinglass jelly, and raisins for dessert, capped off with brandy punch. The women were dressed in their ceremonial best, each with a brightly polished brass band across her forehead and decorated braids to either side of her face. On the breast of each was a ten-inch-square cloth of scarlet fringed with many long strings of beads and glass buttons.

Later in the month, Hall led a party to the ships at Depot Island, where all kinds of entertainment took place. Orations were made on the memory of Franklin and the fate of his expedition. Drama, singing, and farces were enjoyed. Tookoolito exhibited her skill in a Greenland dance.

In March, much of the group broke up, and Hall moved into a new igloo with Ebierbing and Tookoolito. He did this to satisfy the Inuit superstition that since so few of the people now remained in the village, they must abandon all their old huts or risk failure in the seal and walrus hunt. Tookoolito lined the new igloo with the sail and jib of the *Sylvia*, ripped-up canvas bags, and the petticoat she had worn in the United States. It was a time of want and cold, but securing an *oogjook,* or bearded seal, and a walrus saved the day.

On April 15, 1865, Hall finally set out on the journey north to Repulse Bay. He had with him a party of thirteen Inuit. The usual problems of severe weather; snowblindness; ferocious, almost unmanageable dogs; and the constant need to find food prevailed. Every member of the party, including children, had to help pull the five heavily laden sleds through the deep snow.

Hall did not know, of course, that Generals Lee and Grant had met at Appomattox Court House to arrange the surrender of the Army of Northern Virginia, nor that, five days later, on April 14, President Lincoln had been shot in the back of the head by John Wilkes Booth. The tolling bells, saluting guns, and rolling wheels of the presidential funeral train were lost in the crack of ice and the sweep of bitter wind. Far to the west across the top of the world, the Confederate marauder *Shenandoah* had entered the Bering Sea in search of whalers off Alaska. By June, she had captured nineteen ships.

In the late summer of 1865, it became apparent that Tookoolito was pregnant. On September 16, she gave birth to her second son. Hall immediately named him King William, and from then on he was referred to as "Little King William."

After the pregnancy and birth, Tookoolito was under pressure to adhere to numerous taboos. As she sequestered herself and followed customary dietary rules—only stewed caribou meat, no cold water—Hall became increasingly irritated with what he considered backsliding; he had never stopped instructing her in the Bible or looking upon her as an example to her people.

Several months after the birth, Hall and Tookoolito were equally angered by what happened to one of the tribesmen's wives, a woman who was known as Queen Emma. In poor health, Queen Emma was accused of having given birth, secretly, to a tiny dead infant. It was the secrecy, not the stillbirth, that was the infraction. As punishment for her silence, she was sealed in an igloo with her husband and several old women, all bent on revengeful cleansing by restriction of her diet. Hall, helpless, had to stand by as she wasted away and finally died. Disturbed, Tookoolito relented and told Hall she would live as he wished. She agreed to have bread and coffee for the first time since giving birth. She still refused to eat meat, however, saying that she could not eat meat on the same day she had bread and coffee or her child might become sick and die. "How utterly impossible it is to knock or reason these absurd, superstitious ideas out of an Innuit's head," Hall commented. He now saw the Inuit not as people of freedom, able to travel at will, but as prisoners of superstition and taboo. In his journals, his rhetoric swung from a tone of paternal solicitude to one of anger.

On March 31, 1866, Hall set out for King William's Land with Too-koolito, Ebierbing, King William, and three other Inuit families with a total of five children. But soon after they started, a storm struck, and while they were stormbound, King William became ill. They moved on, but the baby's illness worsened. To no avail, Hall continued treating him with podophyllin and asclepin, for pneumonia. Then Nukerzhoo, one of his party, declared himself angakok, reminding Tookoolito that she had been breaking taboos. He told her that for five months she must give up the use of foodstuffs such as bread and tea. There must be no more medicine for the baby. She had no choice but to obey. If she did not, she told Hall, the group would desert him.

They went on—but very slowly, and clearly with no will on the part of the Inuit to reach King William's Land. They expressed foreboding and could not be sped up. Late in April, there was a burst of hope for Hall. He and his party encountered a group from Pelly Bay who were able to give him information about the Franklin party. They even produced relics, including monogrammed silver spoons. But the Pelly Bay natives also told frightening stories of enemies, the Seeneemiutes, who, they said, would attack anyone. Hall knew this was the end; he would have to turn back. He left a cache of food, planning to return.

Hall's trip back to Repulse Bay turned tragic. King William's condition worsened. Pushed to extremes, Tookoolito reverted to the Cumberland Sound custom of desperate parents: to save the child's life by giving it away to another person. An *ankooting*, or ceremony by the angakok, was held to make it official; the next morning Tookoolito handed the sick baby over to the woman who had agreed, earlier, to take him. Soon after, however, Hall insisted that the child be given back; deprived of his mother's milk, he was starving, and Tookoolito was suffering with the milk hardening in her breasts. Another ankooting was held to restore the baby to his mother. But King William could not be saved. He died on May 13.

Tookoolito, distraught, rushed weeping out of the igloo, pressing the dead baby to her breast. Ten minutes later, she returned to her seat on the bed platform, grieving. She held the dead baby for an hour until Mammark, one of the women, could persuade her to allow the body to be wrapped in a furred caribou skin. Custom dictated that the body be buried immediately, but Hall, requesting a day's delay, achieved a compromise. The baby who died at 1:25 in the afternoon was buried at 6:30 that evening.

Following tradition, the body, in its suit of caribou furs, was now wrapped in a blanket of caribou skin of long fur, tied with thongs, and with a loop to go over the neck of the mother, who must carry the corpse. A hole was cut through the wall of the igloo for the funeral procession—Mammark, Tookoolito with the baby's body suspended from her neck, Hall, and Ebierbing. In spite of bitterly cold winds and blowing snow, taboos forbade the mother to dry her socks, repair her boots, or wear her double jacket.

Nukerzhoo, the self-appointed angakok, and Mammark lost no time in berating Tookoolito. The child would have lived, they said, if only she had followed their advice, if only she had not taken back the child, if only she had not departed from the customs of daily living. For one year, she and her husband were to be very careful in regard to what they ate—it must not be raw; and Ebierbing was not to carry on his usual daily duties even in the matter of preparing the ammunition for the hunt.

Hall said that no Inuit tribes are as cursed with so many ridiculous customs as the people of Repulse Bay and the Igloolik people to the north.

But these were the people with whom he was stuck and with whom he would have to go on living and traveling. They were his burden but also his key to any possible success. He prepared to wait out another year before his next attempt on King William's Land.

The summer weather was pleasant, with the temperature in the forties and fifties, and the end of August brought whales and whalers. Hall had been considering traveling with white men only, and when the ships arrived, he made deals with their captains. He would provide Inuit assistance with hunting in the winter if they provided men for him in the spring.

Early in February 1867, Hall left for Igloolik to obtain dogs, a prerequisite for his next venture. After a grueling trip of privation and frustration, he returned to Repulse Bay on March 31—too late; the whaling captains were busy preparing for the season and would allow him no men. Yet another year stretched in front of him. He could not try again for twelve months.

It was a despondent year of half-hearted effort, but there was just enough rumor of white men who could be Franklin survivors to keep him going. He made another trip to Igloolik. Sometime in the spring of 1868, Tookoolito and Ebierbing adopted a child—a little girl born in Igloolik in July 1866. Tookoolito and Ebierbing named the child Punna, which means "little child." She became known as Punny.

It was not at all unusual for Inuit couples to adopt one another's children. Their society was open and inclusive. In this case, however, the father needed some persuasion. Hall provided a sledge. Then, when the deal was concluded, he added some shirts.

A blank spot in Hall's journal, from July 31 to August 21, 1868, shrouds an event that changed his life: He shot an unarmed hired crewman, Patrick Coleman, for "a burst of mutinous conduct." Coleman lingered, horribly, for two weeks before dying, while Hall nursed him. The other hired hands fled. And so ended Hall's efforts to put together a team of white men. He was alone again with the Inuit people to endure another winter, this time plagued by remorse as well as physical discomforts. No legal ramifications came of the shooting; the area where it had occurred was too far away to interest any governmental entity. The incident, however, was a dark turn in his trajectory.

In March 1869, Hall set out for King William's Land once more. This time, he was accompanied by Tookoolito, Ebierbing, and Punny; Ouela; Nukerzhoo and his new wife Ooshoo (the mother of Punny); and "Jerry," with his wife and infant. In spite of the fears regarding the Pelly Bay natives, all went smoothly, and the party reached Rae Strait—directly across from King William's Land—in six weeks. There, Hall was rewarded by tales and relics of the Franklin men that must have made all his years of preparation seem worthwhile. Now he was truly close to the heart of the mystery. He wanted only to push on, cross the strait, and spend the summer on King William's Land. But no, the Inuit said, they would give him only a week. They had to return to Repulse Bay or they would be locked in for the winter. Even Tookoolito and Ebierbing refused. Hall had no choice but to comply.

He moved quickly. On an offshore island, he found a human thigh bone. The next day, on the southeast shore of King William's Land—his object for so long—he found a skeleton. After a ceremony, he packed it up and eventually returned it to England for identification. At places where bones were meant to lie beneath the snow, he held further ceremonies and erected small monuments. He learned more. The local people had refused help to the starving Franklin men: They could not provide enough food for both the strangers and themselves. There were, Hall had to conclude, no survivors. It was time to go back to Repulse Bay. The group now consisted of fifteen persons and a team of eighteen dogs. Ironically, on the way home—over the terrain that had starved the Franklin men—there was copious game. Hall noted how the life of a caribou fawn was "footed out": The hunter, having killed the mother, then chased it down and pressed a foot heavily over the young heart. Musk oxen were in abundance. Geese, partridges, and marmots were also there for the taking.

Settled back at Repulse Bay, Hall was fed by a new dream: The North Pole was now his goal. Everything—all these agonizing years trying to set out to find the Franklin party, all of the frustrations, all of the experiences—was now metamorphosed into this next great challenge.

In the last five years, Hall had sledged over 4,000 miles and rowed and sailed through endless indentations of a wild coastline. Now, he gave away many of his belongings, including the *Sylvia*. On August 13, 1869, he and Tookoolito, Ebierbing, and Punny boarded the whaler *Ansel Gibbs* for New York—where he would begin preparation for the next expedition. As the sails filled, he must have looked with poignancy at the Inuit family beside him—still a family, but a different family. As they left the land of no farewell, they were saying *Terbouetie* deep in their hearts.

Chapter Three

1870–1871

THE *POLARIS* BIDS ADIEU TO THE CIVILIZED WORLD

The Polaris *awaiting the* Congress, *August 10, 1871*

Twice in the summer of 1870, Lady Jane Franklin—the indefatigable widow of the missing explorer—met with Hall, once in Cincinnati and once in New York. She was seventy-eight years old, and her husband's ships had last been seen by white men in the summer of 1845. Hall would continue the search for any evidence, he assured her, but only after he had achieved his goal of the North Pole.

Reunited briefly with his wife and two children, Hall threw himself into a whirlwind of lecturing, lobbying, and traveling in search of support. With his Inuit friends at his side, he made appearances in New York, Brooklyn, Pittsburgh, Cincinnati, and Indianapolis. He arrived in Washington on January 30, 1870, and within a few days called on President Grant. On March 8, a joint resolution regarding a voyage to the arctic regions was introduced in the

House of Representatives and in the Senate. On July 9, 1870, the Senate and the House concurred on an amended resolution with an appropriation of $50,000. Three days later, Grant signed the act and, on July 20, appointed Hall "to command the expedition toward the North Pole." He was to report to the Secretary of the Navy and operate under the authority of the Navy: "All persons attached to the expedition are under your command, and shall, under every circumstance and condition, be subject to the rules, regulations, and laws governing the discipline of the Navy, to be modified, but not increased, by you as the circumstances may in your judgment require." Though he had asked for two, he got one ship—the U.S.S. *Periwinkle*, an old Navy steam tug of 387 tons, 135 feet in length. It was refitted and renamed the *Polaris*.

With his ship and his formal commission, the one-time apprentice blacksmith was now Commander Hall, and the expedition he was ordered to effect was his nation's first to the Pole.

Largely for the sake of Tookoolito and Ebierbing, Hall had smoothed over his rift with Budington. He needed the support of the Budingtons to help care for the Inuit family. He then asked Budington to serve as sailing master of the *Polaris*. Budington agreed but became discouraged with political delays and suddenly sailed off with a whaler to Davis Strait. Hall then offered the captaincy to George Tyson, who had been one of the party to overwinter with Budington in Cumberland Sound in 1851–52 and who was now one of the most experienced captains and navigators in the whaling business. At the time of the invitation, Tyson was committed to a whaling cruise and had to turn down Hall's offer. Then Budington,

George E. Tyson

having met impenetrable ice in Davis Strait, returned home and again accepted the post. Afterward, Tyson's cruise was canceled, and he, too, became available. Hall, who wanted very much to have Tyson along, prevailed upon him to join the expedition, then succeeded in getting the Navy to appoint him, at the last minute, as assistant navigator. It seemed a workable compromise but, in hindsight, was a portent: There were, in effect, two captains— two captains, it would turn out, deeply divided.

The rivals were close in age and shared the career of whaling but came to it from very different directions. Budington, a member of a distinguished whaling family, had gone to sea at the age of thirteen, as a cook aboard a fishing boat plying the coast of the Gulf of Mexico. Tyson, born in New Jersey and educated in New York City, started out as an iron worker who longed for ice. According to Tyson's own account, he was about twenty-one in 1851 when he shipped out on the *McLellan* for Cumberland Sound. Like Hall, he had no relevant training or experience. And, like Hall, his career became quickly bound up with the fortunes of the Budingtons.

After a brief return to iron work, Tyson went back to New London in the spring of 1855 and shipped out as "boat-steerer" on the *George Henry* under the command of James Monroe Budington, Sydney's uncle. While they were caught in the pack ice of Davis Strait, Tyson sighted a vessel traveling on a parallel course and insisted on investigating. Taking a search party across the pack ice—an arduous and dangerous trip that took all day—Tyson discovered that the ship was the *Resolute*, a much-honored Franklin search ship abandoned in the ice on May 15, 1854. Tyson reported: "The decanters of wine, with which the late officers had last regaled themselves, were still sitting on the table, *some of the wine still remaining in the glasses. . . .*" Budington brought the ship home, and eventually it was returned to the Admiralty.

Again, in 1856, Tyson shipped out with James Budington on the *George Henry*, this time as second mate. He made the trip again, as first mate, 1857–58. Apparently the voyages of 1855 and 1856 were financial failures: Excessive ice had precluded sufficient whales. And James Budington was never able to get recompense for salvaging the *Resolute*, though his firm was paid $40,000. According to the Budington family biographer, Richard Walter Nielson, "Tyson apparently bore some sort of animosity to the Budington family. This was possibly due to his and all other officers and crew of the *George Henry* not being paid for the 1855 and 1856 voyages when the agents and owners declared bankruptcy." Tyson, too, seemed unable or unwilling to assimilate into the whaling society of the town he chose as home, New London.

Both Tyson and Sydney Budington were ambitious and unafraid to take on difficult and dangerous tasks. Tyson, however, was more willing to take risks and explore new territory. He was the first to take a whaler up the narrow and challenging waterway of Roes Welcome Sound and take a whale there. Both were suspicious, jealous men ready to impute wrong motives to others. But Budington was given to drink, while Tyson found comfort in a bitter pen. The acerbic record he left not only gave us history otherwise lost but also kept himself afloat. Unlike Budington, Tyson found an outlet for his anger.

Whether it was the dark, cold, dangers, or some unnameable spirit, the Arctic seemed to suck up bravery and spit it out in its opposite form—a paranoid and small-minded envy. Just as refraction altered vision, so did sailing through ice transform emotions. Men who might have been friends in other circumstances quickly became enemies.

There was also a split among the crew of the *Polaris*—a wide divide in nationality, language, and loyalty. A large percentage of those on board were foreign born. Emil Bessels, recently arrived in the United States from Heidelberg, was to be chief scientist and surgeon; Prussian-born Frederick Meyer, who had emigrated to the United States in 1864, was to be meteorologist. Only the third member of the scientific corps, R. W. D. Bryan, as-

tronomer and chaplain, was American by birth. Of the ten seamen, nine were of European origin; they came from Germany, Prussia, Russia, Sweden, Denmark, and England. Later, these demographics would be significant; in retrospect, disastrous. As Loomis points out, it was not at all unusual during this time for the United States Navy and the Merchant Marine to hire immigrants. The Homestead Act had been passed in 1862. Now, with the Civil War over, it was time for another thrust of westward expansion, and many adventuring young men were headed toward the promise of free land and opportunity. The positions they ordinarily would have taken were now being grabbed by immigrants. For another ship, this mix of nationalities might not have made a difference, but for the *Polaris*, with its difficult heading, it was too heavy a load.

During the time of preparation, Tookoolito, Ebierbing, and Punny were in Groton, settling back into what had become their American home. There, they spent time with Captain and Sarah Budington. Tookoolito attended church and Punny started school. A small house and lot were bought for them in the Pleasant Valley Four Corners area near the Budingtons. They made visits to New York to be with Hall and with the Grinnell family, who had been generous supporters. During this time Punny was renamed for Sylvia Grinnell. She was now known as Sylvia Grinnell Ebierbing and was treated kindly by the philanthropist's daughter.

There was no stopping the inexorable movement north. Just as the earth moves counterclockwise around the sun, so was Tookoolito moving counterclockwise, back to the Arctic, back to the swirling black hole of the white man's dreams. She and Ebierbing—and now Punny, too, with her new, weighted name—were in orbit to Hall, and Hall was in sway to the frozen sea. Their new assignment was to reach the North Pole.

On the evening of June 29, 1871, the *Polaris* steamed out of the Brooklyn Navy Yard. The next day, she stopped in New London, where a number of men were replaced: The steward had been discharged for incapacity, and four other men had deserted. One of these was the cook, who was now replaced by William Jackson, an African-American known to Captain Budington. While there, Henry Grinnell presented Hall with a flag from the Wilkes expedition of 1838–40 to Antarctica. That expedition had ended with a court-martial for its commander.

In addition to being beset by a violent thunder and lightning storm on the evening of August 3, the *Polaris* was afire with personal dissensions. Bessels and Meyer had refused Hall's order to sublimate meteorological observations to keeping the ship's official journal. They became the core of the "German faction." (Tyson nearly always referred to the foreign members of the expedition as "Germans," in spite of their heterogeneous backgrounds.) Captain Budington was drinking. Hall had wanted no liquor aboard, but Dr. Bessels had secured some for medical purposes and, it turned out, Budington had brought aboard his own supply of wine. Hall confronted the sailing master, and Budington threatened to resign, "but matters have been smoothed over." Budington was now clearly at odds with both Tyson and Hall.

As they waited at Disko, Greenland, for the supply ship *Congress* to arrive, bringing with it his commission, Tyson remarked: "After seeing what I have, it would suit me just as well if it did not come, for then I should have a decent excuse to return home. There is nothing I should like better than to continue the voyage if all was harmonious, and if each person understood his place and his proper duties."

When the *Congress* did arrive at the anchorage of Godhavn, Hall had to prevail upon its commander, Captain Davenport, and the clergyman, Dr. Newman, who brought prayers for the expedition, to intervene. As Tyson commented:

> *Captain Davenport and Rev. Dr. Newman, who came up in the* Congress, *have had their hands full trying to straighten things out between Captain Hall and the disaffected. Some of the party seem bound to go contrary anyway, and if Hall wants a thing done, that is just what they won't do. There are two parties already, if not three, aboard. All the foreigners hang together, and expressions are freely made that Hall shall not get any credit out of this expedition. Already some have made up their minds how far they will go, and when they will get home again—queer sort of explorers these!*

Davenport, indeed, threatened to take Meyer "home in irons for his insolence and insubordination." But this step would have caused all the "Germans" of the crew to leave, too, destroying the expedition. Before departing, Davenport lectured the crew: Hall was in charge, and all were under Navy discipline.

As the *Congress* pulled away from Godhavn with its authority figures, there were various separations. Her ice pilot, James Budington, was saying goodbye to his nephew, captain of the *Polaris*. Secretly, Hall left behind, in the hands of a local official, all his papers from the second expedition, which he had been planning to edit during his trip to the Pole. As commander of a disaffected crew on the edge of the unknown, he had to weigh his chances.

At a subsequent stop, Upernavik, a well-known Greenland Inuit, Hans Hendrick, came aboard with his wife Mersek, his three children, dogs, and puppies. Now there were two Inuit hunters and their familes on board.

At Tasiussaq, final stop on the coast, more dogs were obtained, for a total of sixty. Here, Hall wrote and sent out his last dispatch that could be carried back to the United States, by way of Denmark. The date was August 24, 1871:

> *The prospects of the expedition are fine; the weather beautiful, clear, and exceptionally warm. Every preparation has been made* to bid farewell to civilization for several years, if need be, *to accomplish our purpose.* . . . *Never was an Arctic expedition more completely fitted out than this.* . . . *The* Polaris *bids adieu to the civilized world.* . . .

Lines of communication cut, the *Polaris* steamed north to adventure, a ship of silence until startling news arrived from Newfoundland on May 9, 1873.

What is our record of that two-year silence and the strange—almost unbelievable—story that emerged from behind the curtain of ice?

Hall's box of journals, letters, notes, and accounts disappeared. There is the official ship's log, mostly an account of weather and observations, essential pages ripped out. There are journals of some of the crew members. (The Navy requested those who could to keep a written account.) There is the record of the Naval Board of Inquiry and the Navy Department's report to Congress for the year 1873. Most significantly, there is the narrative of George Tyson, the last-minute appointment to the staff. His account was published in 1874: *Arctic Experiences: Containing Captain George E. Tyson's*

Tasiusaq, August 13, 1871

Wonderful Drift on the Ice-Floe, a History of the Polaris Expedition, Cruise of the Tigress, and Rescue of the Polaris Survivors, edited by E. (Euphemia) Vale Blake. Commercially unsuccessful, it was never republished. It exists only in Arctic and rare book collections in a small number of libraries in England and the United States and on microfiche.

Tyson's book is overly edited, cautious. It is both truculent and politic. He complains and blames—but usually does not name names. The work was designed to sell. As Loomis points out, the first part—life on board the *Polaris*—is reconstructed from lost notes, and that part, especially, is more a memoir than a journal. It is essential to go beneath the book, into the archives: The National Archives and Records Administration, which houses the Tyson collection in its College Park, Maryland, facility. There, in eight small notebooks written *in situ*, seethe the raw truths of the *Polaris* as Tyson knew them.

In Tyson's account, Tookoolito and Ebierbing suffer. They now become Hannah and Joe. Punny retains her name, probably because it was such a simple one, and Tyson was not much at spelling. Tookoolito receives scant attention, yet she is everywhere. Tyson's lack of focus on her is no reflection of her role but, rather, a reflection of his cultural view. Though she had been to England and had served as Hall's interpreter, she was still, to Tyson, a member of those savage tribes beyond the reach of Christianity. Whereas Hall never stopped proselytizing and hoping for Tookoolito's total conversion, Tyson simply disparaged her shortcomings as those of someone who ought to know better. Without any efforts to instruct her, he kept his distance.

After Davenport, representing the Navy, and Newman, representing God, had left, the conflicted adventurers were on their own. They steamed up Smith Sound, and Kane Basin, reaching the winter quarters of Dr. Elisha Kent Kane's expedition of 1853–55. Then, smooth sailing through icebergs gave way to something else. On August 28, the lookout reported an "impassable barrier of ice." Budington, already hostile to Hall's plans, was clearly afraid. Tyson, however, urged maneuvers to skirt the ice, and the ship went on. They were in waters never before visited by white men, and remarkably good weather enabled them to proceed. While searching for the mythical Open Polar Sea—a concept still widely believed—they entered a narrow basin. This would become Hall Basin. Then came another narrow channel. Hall would name this Robeson Channel for the Secretary of the Navy.

By August 29, ice fields and thick fog impeded the ship's course. Attempts were made to find a harbor. September 2, Hall called a conference with Budington, Tyson, and First Mate Chester. All but Budington wanted to push on. "He [Budington] was very set, and walked off as if to end the discussion. Captain Hall followed him, and stood some time talking to

Passing Fitz Clarence Rock, August 26, 1871

him. . . ." They went no further. Budington's fear, not ice, had become the defining barrier.

The *Polaris* had made 82°11' north—the furthest northing ever and the edge of the eternally frozen Lincoln Sea—one of the nine seas of ice that lead to the Arctic Ocean and the North Pole. She was now drifting south. Winter was closing in and a haven had to be found. September 5, Hall raised an American flag on a bend in the coast. But Repulse Harbor, as he called the bight, offered inadequate shelter. Now they continued drifting south and to the east. On September 10, Hall took refuge on the Greenland coast in what he named Thank God Harbor, anchoring the ship to an iceberg that he designated Providence Berg. The position was latitude 81°38' north, longitude 61°44' west. The *Polaris*, housed in canvas and banked with snow, was now locked in the frozen arms of the arctic winter.

Hunting, surveying, and preparing for the proposed spring sledge trip to the Pole took up the following days. Then, on October 10, Hall, Ebierbing, Hans, and First Mate Chester left with two sledges and fourteen dogs on a preliminary expedition toward the Pole. The commander soon sent back a letter with Hans, asking for a number of items he had forgotten. At the very end, he wrote: "Tell Hannah and little Punny to be good always."

On the afternoon of October 24, Hall and company returned, all well and with no dogs lost. He cheerily greeted, and shook hands with, most of the men, then got out of his fur clothes, and asked for a cup of coffee. After drinking the coffee, brought to him by the English steward, John Herron, Hall was immediately taken sick, vomiting and retching. He went at once to bed. Dr. Bessels, who some reports say was at an onshore observatory where he conducted scientific studies, was summoned. He expressed grave fears for the state of the commander. By eight o'clock, Hall's left side was paralyzed. The doctor announced that his patient had had an apoplectic attack.

Tyson reports:

> . . . *it seems strange, he looked so well. I have been into the cabin to see him. He is lying in his berth, and says he feels sick at his stomach. . . . I think it must be a bilious attack, but it is very sudden. I asked him if he thought he was bilious, and told him I thought an emetic would do him good. He said if it was biliousness it would. Hope he will be better tomorrow.*

But Hall worsened. He became delirious and paranoid.

> *. . . seems to think some one means to poison him; calls for first one and then another, as if he did not know who to trust. When I was in, he accused _____ _____ and _____ _____ of wanting to poison him. When he is more rational he will say, "If I die, you must still go on to the Pole"; and such like remarks. It's a sad affair; what will become of this expedition if Captain Hall dies, I dread to think.*

At one point Hall rallied, but by November 8, he was dead. November 10, he was buried.

A Naval Board of Inquiry would later adopt the conclusion of Dr. Bessels: The commander had died of apoplexy, or stroke. But in 1968, Hall's biographer, Chauncey Loomis, would lead a forensic medical expedition to the commander's lonely grave site. Exhumation and tissue analysis would prove the commander's fears: He had experienced "an intake of considerable amounts of arsenic . . . in the last two weeks of his life."

As Loomis points out, arsenic may or may not have been the primary cause of Hall's death. He might have had a stroke and been medicated—even by himself—with arsenic, part of the day's medical kit. But then again, he might well have been killed by arsenic. His health, apparently, was destroyed with that mysterious cup of coffee, which, he had complained to Tookoolito, was too sweet.

Going back to the testimony before the Board of Inquiry, one finds three obvious suspects: Emil Bessels, Frederick Meyer, and Captain Budington. Each was quoted as expressing relief at the commander's death. Bessels even laughed. Each perceived he had a score to settle with the victim and wanted him out of the way. The "Germans" thought Hall a fool and disputed his command. Budington feared his agenda and wanted to go home. But then, what of the cook? And of the steward? And was Bessels on board the ship at the time, or in the observatory?

Loomis concludes:

> *What happened aboard the USS* Polaris *between October 24 and November 8, 1871, can never be entirely known. What went on in the minds*

*of Hall, Bessels, and the others aboard that ship, and what they did
furtively on their own, is done, gone, past. . . . One way or the other,
Charles Francis Hall died, as his friend Penn Clarke said he would, a
victim of his own zeal.*

My suspicions lean toward Budington, though, at the same time, it is hard
to find in him the craftiness necessary to kill. Budington's tangled history
with Hall goes back many years, while Bessels and Meyer were previously
unknown to him. Budington's antagonism was based not on intellectual ar-
rogance, as was that of Bessels and Meyer; it was seated in much deeper,
more complex emotional depths, and it was fed by alcohol. He had an ally in
the cook, who could well have been an effective accomplice. Budington's actions later, moreover, are highly suggestive of culpability. If he did not kill
Hall, he certainly killed his expedition and put all at peril. At the very least,
he can be justifiably accused of reckless endangerment.

What followed the death was a time of darkness, alcoholic drift (now
Tyson was drinking, too), jealousy, paranoia, and even madness. The expedition was falling apart on every level. No one—and everyone—was in control,
as Ebierbing later testified. Budington refused to take charge and maintain
order. Lack of discipline and exercise let loose the demons of toxic energy.

The Polaris *adrift, November 21, 1871*

The fury of the roiling arctic night was closing in, tighter and tighter: a pressure that perhaps no human mind can truly withstand.

Like the enchanted ship of the Ancient Mariner, the *Polaris* was now borne by powers beyond human sight or control. Weighted by a suspicious death for which there was no confession or repentance, there could be no atonement. Shrouded by depression, lost in isolation, the ship and her crew were now carried into a mysterious fate by currents too deep to fathom.

Chapter Four

✳

November 11, 1871–October 24, 1872

SEPARATION: THE DRIFT BEGINS

The Polaris *near Providence Berg, November 21, 1871*

Commander Hall was given as careful a Christian burial as could be carried out under the circumstances. It took Tyson and a number of men two days to hack out of the frozen earth a shallow resting place for the pine coffin. Hall was faced east—in accordance with the Resurrection—his back to the ice-solid bay. Mr. Bryan, the chaplain, read the Episcopal Service for the Dead. Later, a willow plant, the universal symbol of mourning, was placed on the mound.

The command passed to Captain Budington, who soon disbanded Sunday services with the comment, "Each one could pray for himself just as well." Storms increased, and frostbite threatened everywhere. The pack ice pressed against Providence Berg so hard, it split, lifting and straining the *Polaris*. So great was the strain that it seemed prudent to send the women and children temporarily to the onshore observatory.

Days and weeks passed. Thanksgiving—remembered at table but in no other way—gave way to Christmas. The *Polaris* continued to rise and fall with the tide, her stem resting on the foot of the iceberg. Leaks might have been caulked; the ship might even have been hauled off the iceberg, but Budington gave no orders. Eventually, blasting was tried to break up the foot of the iceberg, but with no success.

A *paraselene*—three moons showing besides the true one—arranged to form a cross in the sky while shooting stars and the northern lights lit up the darkness. As day was swallowed up by night and more attention was given to the heavenly bodies, the men caroused and knew no regular hours. Arms were handed out, but not to Tyson. He alone went unarmed. By Christmas Eve, he noted: "Captain Hall did not always act with the clearest judgment, but *it was heaven to this.*"

The New Year brought no cheer but only colder temperatures and more severe weather. The hapless crew of the *Polaris* had not seen the sun for eighty days. They were heartened during a twenty-four-hour period, January 6–7, 1872, when the aurora borealis kept up an uninterrupted display. The

Thank God Harbor, April 10, 1872

temperature stood at forty-eight degrees below zero.

Eventually, twilight began to show in the southeast quarter. Ebierbing and Hans started to hunt for seals, which could be heard under the ice, making their breathing holes. Daylight was creeping into the dark; it was possible to read outside without a light at midday for short periods. On February 28, the sun rose above the horizon for the first time in 135 days. But all the while, gales lashed for two or three days at a time.

By March, the phenomenon of

Tookoolito at Hall's grave

mock moons had become one of mock suns, with a parhelion of three false suns surrounding the true. Birds returned. Ptarmigans became prey. Both hunting and exploring parties were now going out from the ship on a regular basis, but all activity was random, and surveys made were for the most part repetitions of earlier ones. Captain Budington would not allow an attempt to be made at the Pole. Like another form of ice, he kept the expedition frozen in place.

On April 8, Ebriebing shot a ferocious polar bear that had injured the plucky dog "Bear" and another dog, which was left for dead but recovered. Musk ox hunting provided sport and fresh meat. Ebierbing and Hans came back from one hunt with seven; three had to be left behind in the igloo they built because the dogs could haul only four.

Tyson was becoming increasingly concerned about Budington's plans and motivations. On May 1, he requested of the captain permission to make a sledge trip north. Budington said it was not practical. A gale slammed the ship against the iceberg, causing her to careen. On May 9, in spite of Budington's statements to the contrary, Tyson started north with a sledge party consisting of Meyer, Ebierbing, and Hans. They reached Newman Bay and as far north as 82°9'. By May 20, the snow was disappearing from the mountains and the pack ice softening. Early in June, the *Polaris*, rising from the melting ice, sprang a new leak on the starboard side where two planks were badly split. More attention had to be given to pumping. Two boat parties were arranged for another expedition to Newman Bay. Two days after leaving, First Mate Chester was back with his group: They had lost their boat, crushed when a heavy floe, moving in against the shore, shattered an iceberg on top of it. Tyson, fully appreciative of the potential need for small boats, named the site Cape Disaster.

On land, summer was more evident. Willows, growing like vines, could be seen along with mosses and flowers. Tyson and Chester wanted to continue north, to reach 83°, but Budington said he would not wait for them; if he got a chance to break free of the ice, he would leave immediately—and wait for no one.

On July 4, the captain ordered the hunting and exploring parties back to the ship; he hoped at any moment to be able to make the break. Final repairs were begun on Hall's grave. July 24, a gale blew much of the ice out of the bay, but the *Polaris* was still taking on water, and additional effort had to be given to pumping. The repairs on the grave continued. Chester got a board and carved out the inscription, replacing the former marker with the lines written in pencil. A crowbar was left thrust at the head of the mound.

August 12, 1872, was a memorable day. Mersek gave birth to a baby boy. Tyson recorded in his journal some of the "savage" customs she observed, namely giving birth alone and severing the umbilical cord with her teeth, and destroying the clothes she wore during the birth. By acclamation, the infant was named "Charlie Polaris."

The surprise birth of Charlie Polaris presaged a hopeful event: Later in the day, with the ice opening and a good lead of water appearing, the *Polaris* steamed out of her winter prison. Just as the vessel lurched forward, one of the best dogs, a Newfoundland named Tiger, leaped over the bulwarks and was lost on the ice. For the ship, it was a short-lived freedom. Three days later, the *Polaris* was trapped again, anchored to a floe, drifting south with the current.

Narwhals, tusked grayish-white whales that usually indicated breaks in the ice, appeared, but no leads opened. Fog descended. The ship, steered by no mortal man but by invisible powers beneath the ice, continued her involuntary voyage, pumps going.

August turned to September, and once more, the light began to shorten. The ship was drifting south at a rate of about ten miles a week. Seals and walruses were seen. The coal supply became dangerously low. On October 4, the ship passed Dr. Kane's winter quarters of 1853–55, the ice groaning around them. There was little hope of getting home this season, and preparations had to be made for another winter. While Ebierbing and Hans hunted seal, Tyson began work on a hut on the ice in which to store provisions.

Then, at 6:00 P.M. on October 15, 1872, a strong gale blew up out of the northwest, and the ice began to nip the ship. The *Polaris* rose and fell with the pressure, groaning and creaking. The engineer, Emil Schumann, came running from below among the startled crew shouting that "the vessel had started a leak aft and that the water was gaining on the pumps." When Tyson reported this to Budington, the captain threw up his arms and yelled out to "throw everything on the ice!" Wrote Tyson:

> *Instantly everything was confusion, the men seizing everything indiscriminately, and throwing it overboard. These things had previously been placed upon the deck in anticipation of such a catastrophe; but as the vessel, by its rising and falling motion, was constantly breaking the ice, and as no care was taken how or where the things were thrown, I got overboard, calling some of the men to help me, and tried to move what I could*

Winter quarters by Providence Berg, April 17, 1872

away from the ship, so it should not be crushed and lost; and also called
out to the men on board to stop throwing things till we could get the things
already endangered out of the way; but still much ran under the ship.

Later, the engineer's statement was found to be false. No additional leak
had occurred. Because of the movement of the ship on the ice, the water in
the hold sloshed in such a way that it appeared that new water was rushing
in. Tyson, who had reboarded, was now convinced the ship was sound. Leaving Budington and thirteen other men on board, he went back out on the ice
to try to save the provisions being thrown down helter-skelter. He worked
alongside Tookoolito. But soon the ice exploded under their feet, and *"the*
ship broke away in the darkness, and we lost sight of her in a moment."
      Gone! Adrift in the arctic night!
      Snowing and blowing sleet so powerfully that no one could look to wind-
ward, it was hardly possible to know what had happened—and certainly not
possible to know who was on the ice and who was on the ship when it broke
away and disappeared in the storm. Just as the break came, Tyson pulled
away from the ship some musk ox skins that were lying across a wide crack
in the ice. To his amazement, he discovered "two or three" of Hans's children
rolled up in one of the skins.
      Tyson and some of the men used whale boats to bring everyone they
could find to firm ice. Not knowing the extent of the piece they were on,
they settled down as best they could, wrapping themselves in musk ox skins,
to wait for first light. Tyson alone walked the floe all night.
      Dawn brought clear weather and some answers but no relief. Huge ice-
bergs, obviously, had pressed upon the ice floe until it exploded. Beyond the
ice, there were leads, but no sight of the *Polaris*. The floe on which Tyson
found himself was circular, about four miles in circumference, and rough,
with ponds and thirty-foot-thick hillocks. Now he began to count his party.
Some were still on smaller floes and had to be rescued. The others were
buried in snow. Finally, he accounted for eighteen persons:

Frederick Meyer, meteorologist: born in Prussia, in the United States since
      1864
John Herron, steward: born Liverpool, United States citizen
William Jackson, cook: 25, African American, born in New York

Seamen:
> *John W. C. ("Robert") Kruger: 29, born in Germany, not a United*
> *   States citizen*
> *Frederick Jamka: 23, born in Prussia*
> *William Linderman: 23, born in Germany*
> *Frederick Aunting: born in Russia, on the Prussian border*
> *Gustavus W. Lindquist: 26, born in Stockholm*
> *Peter Johnson: 33, born in Denmark, in United States 8 or 9 years*

Inuit:
> *Tookoolito, Ebierbing, and Punny*
> *Hans, Mersek, and their four children: Augustina, Tobias, Succi, and*
> *   Charlie Polaris (eight weeks old)*

George E. Tyson at this point became Captain Tyson, filling the role he had almost held before the *Polaris* set sail. But now he was captain of an ice floe adrift in one of the most dangerous bodies of water in the world; and his accidental crew, one of the most polyglot and ill-matched that ever a captain came to command.

Tyson had only the clothes on his back—not even a coat—and no gun. He also had enormous arctic experience, a level head, a sense of fairness, and a determination to do right by the group for whom he had so strangely and suddenly become responsible. He had a depth of decency and discipline that would more than make up for his lack of winter garments and equipment. He might not have chosen the post, but it is fortunate that fate had chosen him.

Fate, indeed, might have been preparing him for the post for two decades. Already he had had twenty-three years of experience sailing the northern and arctic seas. He had not celebrated a Fourth of July at home in the United States for twenty years. (Whaling captains often commented on how they missed summer and its pleasures, such as fresh strawberries and cream.) He had learned about ice and he had learned about seals—an education that would prove vital in the coming months.

Tyson knew that the first order of business on board the ice floe was checking food supplies. What did they have? Fourteen cans of pemmican, eleven and a half bags of ship's bread, one can of dried apples, fourteen hams, and a small store of chocolate. This was more than it seems. The cans were large—the pemmican cans weighed 45 pounds and the apple, 22. The bags of ship's bread, or hard biscuit, weighed 133 pounds.

Most important, there were two eight-man whale boats.

These boats now had to be prepared and the party put aboard for an attempt to reach either the *Polaris* or land—and possibly some helpful natives. Tyson's crew, however, was inert, claiming that they were hungry and tired and wet. They had to build a fire from pieces of wood they found on the ice and attempt to cook a meal. By nine o'clock, the leads were closing and the wind shifting. An attempt to reach land failed. Then, the *Polaris* was spotted, approximately ten miles away. Tyson put up a flag and watched through his spy glass. She was under steam and sail, but instead of coming toward them, she dropped away. Tyson was dumbfounded. Later, she was seen again, tied up. That was the last glance of what represented home and hope. The ice floe began drifting. Tyson was desperate; at any moment they could be frozen in. He threw away everything he could in order to lighten the two boats and ordered the men to "start immediately." Only murmuring, muttering, and grumbling ensued:

> *The men did not seem to realize the crisis at all. They seemed to think more of saving their clothes than their lives. But I seemed to see the whole winter before me. Either, I thought, the* Polaris *is disabled and cannot come for us, or else, God knows why, Captain Budington don't mean to help us. . . . Then the thought came to me, what shall I do with all these people, if God means we are to shift for ourselves, without ship, or shelter, or sufficient food, through the long, cold, dark winter?*

Tyson's fears would soon be realized. The men, who had known no discipline since Hall's death, insisted on loading everything they could into one boat—which had to be dragged across the floe to be launched. In a sudden storm, no one would follow him but William Jackson, the cook, who went back for the others. Then, when the boat was finally brought to the edge of the floe, Tyson found only three oars and no rudder! He persisted. The boat was launched into a furious wind, but they were immediately thrown back on the ice. Everyone was exhausted. Darkness fell, the day was lost, and, with it, their last opportunity to strike out for the *Polaris*, which, it seemed,

The parting of the ship's company, October 15, 1872

was not going to come for them. Tyson, at the end of his strength, left the boat on the edge of the ice and returned to the center of the floe. There he put up a tent, ate a little frozen meat and ship's bread, and fell asleep for the first time in many hours.

His sleep was short. He awoke to cries from the Inuit: The ice had broken, separating them from their boat. Also on that severed piece of the floe was the hut Tyson had originally built—and, inside it, six bags of ship's bread. Tyson's compass was in the boat. The piece of ice on which the party now drifted was one hundred and fifty yards across each way. Storms and heavy seas ate away at it hour by hour. Several days later, Ebierbing spied the lost boat on the other, larger floe. With the help of six dogs, Tyson and Ebierbing saved the boat and the bread. They now had both boats, as well as two kyacks that belonged to Ebierbing and Hans.

For more than a week, as they settled down on the crowded shard of their original ice floe, the abandoned party kept looking and waiting for the *Polaris*. But by October 23, all hope of rescue had been abandoned. They were on their own. Now it was a question of figuring out how to get to land. There were no sledges, only the boats, which had to be dragged over rough ice. First, it was necessary to regain the larger floe, and they did this with great difficulty. Then, when all was rescued but the kyacks—indispensable to Inuit hunters—Jackson and Linderman ventured back with Ebierbing and Hans to the smaller floe. During this process, one of the kyacks was saved but the other lost.

One kyack, two eight-man boats, pemmican, dried apples, hams, bread, and nineteen cold, hungry people on a large ice floe. Now it was time to settle down—to wait and attempt to survive. The *Polaris* would not come. Nothing would come but darkness and worse weather. They were alone and abandoned in the arctic night, prisoners of the pack ice, vassals of the polar spirits.

Ebierbing and Hans built a small village of igloos, Ebierbing doing most of the work. There was an igloo for Tyson and Meyer; one for Ebierbing and his family; one for the men; a storehouse; and a cook house. These were all united by arched alleyways. Hans built an igloo for his family that was separate but nearby.

The igloos were built as always: quickly and efficiently, within an hour or two. The igloo-builder would plunge his long bone snow knife into several banks of snow in order to find the proper compactness. He would then cut blocks two feet to two and one-half feet in length and eighteen inches in thickness. One set is cut from the spot on which the igloo is to be built, its floor being thus eighteen inches below the general surface. In placing the blocks around this excavation, of about ten feet in diameter, the first tier is made up of those, which, by increasing regularly in width, form a spiral from right to left. They are laid from within, each being secured by a bevel on the one last laid and another bevel on the next one below. The blocks incline inwardly, thus regularly diminishing the diameter of the igloo and fitting it for the dome or keystone. For ventilation, a small hole is usually made by a spear. The crevices are well filled with snow within and without, making the ice hut nearly airtight. For a window, a small opening cut in the dome is filled in, usually with a block of clear ice or with the scraped membranes of a seal. The entryway is long and points toward the south, so low that one almost has to crawl in. The farthest end from the entry is slightly raised and represents parlor and bedroom, the front part workshop and kitchen. Snow is banked up over the igloo once it is built.

Tyson's group created a substitute for the traditional Inuit stone lamp out of an old pemmican can with pieces of canvas for wicking. This system worked for all but the men, who started breaking up one of the boats for fuel. Tyson was alarmed: "These boats are not designed to carry more than six or eight men, and yet I foresee that all this company may have yet to get into the one boat to save our lives, for the ice is very treacherous."

Taking stock of their goods, Tyson determined that they did not have enough food to keep nineteen people alive on the floe until April or May, when he estimated that they would drift into the whaling grounds. The party was down to two carefully apportioned meals a day—eleven ounces total per day for each adult, half rations for the children. Meyer constructed scales to ensure fairness, but pilfering had already started, especially of the chocolate. There was no way, given the conditions, to guard the storehouse. Hans killed two of the dogs for his family, an act that incensed Tyson's anti-Inuit sentiments and caused him to rail against what he perceived as improvidence and greed.

The party grew weak. "I am so weak myself," Tyson commented, "that I stagger from sheer want of strength. . . ." The ice held them in its groaning arms. The captives' floe was eight or ten miles offshore at what Tyson estimated to be 77°30' north.

Never would they be sure of where they were; they had no charts and little in the way of instruments. Instinct vied with desire and distorted calculations. They could be certain only that powerful currents were carrying them south—a dark and starving village on the skin of the frozen sea, and that eventually they would melt into the open water near Labrador. With their supplies dwindling, all that could save them now was the flesh and blood of the seal.

Chapter Five

October 26, 1872–November 28, 1872

A GIFT OF SEALS

Tookoolito had married an extraordinarily skilled hunter. Ebierbing's skill was secondary only to his dedication and his patience: Hall had seen him spend hours, even days, waiting motionless on the ice at the breathing hole of a seal. And when he failed to secure his prey, he would go back again and again—often on the verge of starvation.

It was important to be married to a good hunter. And back in Cumberland Sound, Tookoolito had wanted to stay married. Ebierbing was older than she and had been married before. His uncle, the powerful and successful Ugarng of Frobisher Bay, had had thirteen wives by the time Hall met him in 1860. He was eager for his nephew to take another wife.

The possibility of a hunter's taking another wife was always there and, in the case of Tookoolito, strongly so because of her husband's prowess. One of the reasons Tookoolito was anxious to accompany Hall to the United States the first time was to remove Ebierbing from the temptation. She had learned enough of Christian ways to know that monogamy was an option and respectful treatment within marriage possible. By the end of the second expedition with Hall, Ebierbing was quite openly taking other women with him on hunting trips, sometimes in accompaniment with Tookoolito. According to Hall, Tookoolito claimed she would "prefer to die right away rather than stay home and be abused as she knows she must be, if no white men are about."

Among her people, such arrangements—less permanent than marriage—were ordinary practices. Exchange of wives was common among the people of Baffin Island and, given the context, sensible. The practice helped forge bonds of friendship and maintained communal strength. If, for instance, a man needed to travel and his wife could not accompany him because of illness or pregnancy, he could "borrow" another man's wife, who, indeed, might wish to travel to the same place to visit relatives. Crafty angakoks often took advantage of the practice, however, demanding exchange as part of their tribute.

Outside the bounds of Christianity, monogamy was not a large issue; and, within the tupic or igloo, sex was hardly a private matter. Privacy in undressing was a protected right—it was not seemly to watch a person disrobe, and everyone undressed before getting under the caribou skins on the sleeping platform at the rear of the igloo. But what happened under the skins could hardly be kept from notice, not when numerous sleepers were packed side by side into a space with a diameter of ten feet. There was no need nor expectation of privacy when privacy was almost unknown. Privacy, indeed, could easily be fatal in a situation where group strength was critical. To be alone—to be isolated—was to die. A punitive edict of banishment was a death warrant. The individual who could not add to the strength of the whole—whether it was an infant girl considered superfluous or an incapacitated adult—would be deserted and left to die. The good of the whole was paramount; community was everything.

According to Hall, Tookoolito had been impressed with the biblical story of Joseph, which he had read to her during one of her illnesses. It must have been Matthew's version: the account of the just and submissive man who accepts the news, in a dream, that his betrothed is pregnant by a mysterious

source, the Holy Ghost. Tookoolito, married in England in the Christian rite
but still practicing the ways of her people, must have wanted very much to
know that such marital devotion is possible: that a man might give his full
and unquestioning protection to a woman so strangely touched, without
doubt and without anger. While both the Holy Ghost and the angakok were
strange and powerful, the Holy Ghost seemed to demand gentleness and acceptance while the angakok often demanded payment and punishment.
How could her husband be brought to understand the new and temperate
ways?

Ebierbing was devoted, but it was to the discipline of hunting and providing for his people. Tookoolito, in turn, was devoted to the memory of her
deceased employer and friend, Father Hall. Their combined dedication to
practical needs and moral principles created a powerful, cohesive energy
that would be critical to the salvation of all the ice floe prisoners. It was syn-
ergy enough to hold their small and oscillating ice world together.

It was now October 26, eleven days since—what was it to be called—the
Separation? the Casting Away? the Desertion? The prisoners were starved
for light as well as food: the sun was almost entirely gone, showing at most
seven feet above the horizon. It would soon be totally out of view and would
not return for three months.

Ebierbing and Hans had been hunting, so far without success. They had
with them the dogs, harnessed to the sled. If the men encountered a polar
bear, the dogs would keep it at bay until the men could get a shot at it. A polar bear, though dangerous, could provide abundant provisions. By October
30, no seals had appeared, and the dogs were starving. Tyson determined that
they would have to be done away with—but not just yet.

Seals live principally under the ice and can be seen and pursued only
when the ice cracks in milder weather. As mammals, dependent on air, they
make holes through ice and snow in order to breathe. These holes are no
more than two and a half inches across—very difficult for the human eye to
detect, particularly in the dim and uncertain light in which Ebierbing and
Hans were working. Moreover, seals are extremely shy and sensitive, seem-
ing to know when they are being watched. A seal hunter would sometimes
remain on guard at an air hole for thirty-six or forty-eight hours before getting a chance to strike; and, if the first blow failed, there would not be a
second chance. The hunter would use a barbed spear with line attached:

a small, specially crafted harpoon. If the strike was well aimed, the spear would penetrate the thin skull of the seal and secure it until the hunter could enlarge the hole sufficiently to pull the body through.

During their eleven years together, Ebierbing had repeatedly exhibited to Hall the extraordinary patience and attention to detail that seal hunting on the ice required. Once Hall watched as Ebierbing removed from the hole he had made in the ice a small hair that had fallen from his caribou jacket. Of this, he remarked to Hall, ". . . smell um quick, and away it go."

Seals, sea lions, and walruses make up the order Pinnipedia, or fin-footed, mammals. Unlike cetaceans—the other major group of marine mammals that includes whales and dolphins—pinnipeds must return to land or ice to give birth to their young and care for them. Excellent swimmers with the ability to dive deeply, pinnipeds are protected from cold by a thick layer of fat, or blubber, just under the skin. Though they live in all seas except the northern part of the Indian Ocean, pinnipeds are most abundant in colder waters.

There are two families of seals: the Otariidae, or eared seals, and the Phocidae, or earless seals. Of these latter, more streamlined seals, those relevant to the ice floe party were the harbor seal; ringed seal; bearded seal; and hooded or crested seal. Bearded seals can grow to 10 feet in length and 900 pounds, while hooded seals can be up to 12 feet and 1,000 pounds. The capture of either would mean abundant supplies of food and oil.

At a distance, cow seals and their pups recognize one another by unique calls and, at closer range, by unique scents. The males of both the bearded and the ringed seal species call underwater. The bearded seal male is said to produce a distinctive underwater song.

Such vocalizations are not the only aspect that makes seals appear, at times, eerily human. Their gestation period is nine months and their life span around twenty-five years. One ringed seal, a female, is known to have lived forty-three years. Cows give birth, usually, to one pup; twins are rare. A mother is never in doubt as to which pup is hers and stays with it closely through the lactation period, which differs in time according to the relative safety of the breeding site. In spite of their saltwater environment, they breathe air through lungs, drink fresh water, and move, though haltingly, on land. They are curious, drawn to music and unusual sounds, and are sociable. When sailors saw a large shoal of ringed seals springing up together for air, sometimes with their whole bodies out of the water, they would call the phenomenon a "seal's wedding."

Most strikingly, when a female ringed seal is preparing to give birth in the spring, she uses her claws to create a lair out of snow on the pack ice. It is a dwelling so similar to the igloo that the Inuit call it a seal igloo, or *agloo*. Dome-shaped and five feet in diameter, it is two-and-a-half feet high, with a depth of snow above it of some five feet to protect it from sharp-scented animals. There is a platform on one side where the seal gives birth and nurses the pup. Two inches below the platform laps the water leading to the passageway down through the sea ice. The nursing pup stays with its mother in the den for approximately six weeks, when sun begins to melt the snow cover and the dome collapses.

From the earliest time of storytelling on northern coasts, seals have been considered the link between sea and land, water and earth. In Celtic lore, they are part of the shadowy kingdom of merfolk and selkies—those half-aquatic, half-human creatures who manifest the magic of metamorphosis. Cry seven times by a shore, and a seal will answer. Fall carelessly in love, and your beloved will forsake you for an alien seal world, leaving you heartbroken on a rock-strewn beach.

Farther north, in the Inuit culture of Baffin Island, the connection goes to a more profound level—a view that animal and human life are inextricably bound and kept in balance with one another by mutual respect and carefully observed taboos. With this perspective, little separates people from animals. All life forms can change place with one another and travel by disguise. According to Inuit beliefs, to have animals for tools, sleds, and clothing and food, building materials for housing, necessitates keeping in perfect equilibrium with them; and that equilibrium is dependent on keeping a peaceful relationship with the power that regulates them.

That power is Sedna, the goddess-under-the-sea, who controls the animals of the deep and is the daughter of Anguta, chief deity. It is she, the secondary divinity, who sends—or does not send—seals, walrus, and whales to be caught. It is she to whom the angakok must travel and make supplication in hungry times. Sedna was said to be a girl who refused to marry but who finally took as her husband a deceitful petrel. When her father carried her back from the petrel's home in his boat, the petrel caused a heavy gale, and Sedna's father threw her overboard to save himself. When she clung to the boat, he cut off the joints of her fingers, which became whales and seals, and then knocked out one of her eyes. She descended to the lower world, to live in a house of stone and whale rib, and from there she rules the sea mammals. A dog, said to be her husband, stands guard at the door. Her father also lives with her.

Father, daughter, guard dog: Here in this watery other world resides redemption. The daughter has given her life that the people might live. They eat of her body and flesh, but only through successful supplication. Was this cycle really so different from that of the whalers' Christ?

For the Christian foreigners, there was nothing mystical under the sea. European seal hunters, who started sailing into the northern waters as early as the Middle Ages, were in a hurry. While the Inuit method of killing seals was time and labor intensive, it was different for Europeans. Writing in 1820, the eminent British whaler and naturalist William Scoresb Jr. noted how lucrative the harvest could be: A sealer could occasionally in the month of April alone procure as many as 4,000 to 5,000 seals, yielding nearly 100 tons of oil. The method was clubbing and skinning, the slaughter fast. So tenacious of life are the seals, Scoresby remarked, that he has seen them swim after being flayed, "when in a state too shockingly mangled to be fit for description."

For the Inuit of Baffin Island, the taking of a seal requires a careful ritual: A few drops of water are sprinkled on its head before it is cut up. This is to thank the seal and provide it the symbol of a life-giving drink, encouraging its kind to keep returning; seals need fresh water to drink as much as their human hunters. If there is no water to be had, the hunter holds snow in his hands until he squeezes out a single drop. Women are not allowed to eat of the first seal of the season—not even to the extent of chewing the blubber for the sake of expressing oil. If oil is needed, a man must pound the blubber.

On the *Polaris* ice floe, everything was wrong. It was winter, not the season for seals, and no rituals could make it right. Still, seals had to be found and captured or all would die. The hunt continued from darkness to darkness.

On November 1, two weeks after the Separation, an attempt was made to reach shore. The boat was loaded with provisions and dragged halfway to the edge of the floe. Then the ice broke, and the dogs and sled were almost lost. The castaways were prevented from becoming runaways. Bad weather set in, and the village of igloos had to be rebuilt. Tookoolito must have been both disheartened and relieved to have the task—the familiar activity she had been repeating all her life, her hands quickly putting things to right; and now, with so little, it was a process stripped to the basics. Tyson stayed sick in bed for three days. Without adequate clothing, he suffered constantly from the cold and on and off with bouts of rheumatism.

Finally, on November 6, Ebierbing shot and secured a seal. "We are all prisoners," Tyson said; but they had been given a reprieve from their death sentence. Four days later, when Ebierbing and Hans set out to hunt once more, they became separated, and Hans did not return that night. Ebierbing and Robert Kruger went out to look for him. At one point, seeing what they thought was a polar bear coming at them, they loaded their pistols. Luckily, they held their fire until the creature got closer: It was Hans, his fur clothing covered with snow, climbing over hummocks.

November 15: One month exactly since the Terrible Night, the Gale, the Separation. The weather had cleared, the sky washed with moonlight. The nineteen ice-wanderers were still together, locked in the arctic night. The dogs had fared less well. Five had been shot; four remained, and they were suffering. There was nothing to feed them. Fox trails led only to frustration.

By November 19, Tyson was sick again, crippled with rheumatism, hardly able to pick up his pencil but still managing to record the efforts of the hunters. Two bear tracks and five seal holes were observed but no meat brought back. The only light for hunting now was moonlight—on those nights when it was clear. The second boat had been completely cut up and burned. Tyson was determined to protect the remaining boat, with his life, if need be. He knew that, eventually, the current would carry them beyond the ice. The only fuel now was seal oil. Without seal, there would be no fuel, no fire, no chance for any warmth or cheer.

Meyer, the meteorologist, was suffering particularly, finding it difficult to walk. He moved in with the men, among whom German was largely the language spoken. Tyson, in turn, moved in with Tookoolito, Ebierbing, and Punny, with whom he could speak English. With Hans and Mersek in their own igloo, there were now three residences, each with a different primary language.

On November 21, Ebierbing brought in two seals—and immediate relief. Tyson recorded:

For the first time since separating from the ship I have eaten enough; *but it was of raw, uncooked seal-meat—skin, hair, and all. For the last few days, being sick, I had eaten nothing—scarcely any thing for about a week; and I was so very weak on getting up I found I could hardly stand; and I needed this food very much to give me a little strength . . . this one night I have eaten heartily of seal—yes, and drank its blood, and eaten its blubber, and it will give me strength, I hope. I need strength for many reasons besides my own use.*

Tyson had partaken of the communion. The body and blood of the seal were now his body and blood. He lived with the man who provided it, depending on the man's wife to make, repair, and maintain the clothing the hunter required. The woman depended on the man to bring home the oil by which she might make light to do her work and the food needed to fuel her body. Tyson was now part of this ancient symbiosis. What he had so often referred to in his journals as "civilization" had dropped away. Nothing mattered but the balance of primordial interdependency: seal, man, and woman bound together on the icy skin of the sea in a delicate and dangerous dance.

Once, long ago, in what must have seemed another lifetime, Tyson had tried to make a pet of a young seal. It was the winter of 1851–52 as he waited for the spring whales to come to Tookoolito's island in Cumberland Sound. It was a hard winter—a winter of short provisions that turned into a year of want—and he was a lonely colonist far from home. He had found and carried back to his hut an orphaned seal pup and left it outside while he went inside for a hurried supper. When he came out again, eager to care for his pet, he discovered that the seal had been crushed by the boot of a fellow whaler.

The loneliness of the Arctic had caused other expeditions to turn to animals for companionship, not just sustenance. The ice journals are dotted with dogs and cats, sometimes canaries and linnets; and in one instance, a duck that had the misfortune of angering the captain who insisted on its decapitation.

Men aboard the *Emma* overwintering in Cumberland Sound during 1859–60 captured a fox and kept it in a cage. In May 1872, while the *Polaris* was trapped in the ice, Robert Kruger brought to the ship a live lemming, which was put into a box and "carefully fed." Soon he added another one. In July, another two lemmings were caught for which, according to *Polaris* editor C. H. Davis, "the sailors rigged a cage on top of the galley. This cage had glass sides and many little retreats; and much interest was shown in watching the little creatures and in feeding them."

For the Inuit, however, pets were not viable. Puppies, perhaps. Children played with puppies—quickly put into small harnesses—and toy sleds. They also played with toy harpoons and spears; hunting was practiced from a young age, and what they hunted were seals. Sentimentality could not be afforded.

On November 21, the day of the seal feast on the ice, two dogs got at the provisions and were shot. Two dogs remained.

Thanksgiving came to the prisoners on the floe, marked not by feasting but by hunger. What was left of the can of dried apples had been saved for the occasion. Tyson's breakfast, eaten at noon, consisted of a small meat can full of chocolate and two biscuits. To satisfy his fierce hunger, Tyson finished his meal with frozen seal blubber and strips of frozen seals' entrails and seal skin, hair and all, just warmed over the lamp. For dinner, Tyson, Tookoolito, Ebierbing, and Punny shared six biscuits; one pound of canned meat; a one-pound can of corn; and one of mock-turtle soup. Tookoolito took all of these ingredients, mixed them together in one of the few flat pans available, and warmed the mixture over the lamp. Empty cans served as dishes. Nearby, in their crowded igloo, the nine crewmen had the same ingredients for their dinner, as did Hans and his family in theirs.

There was no formal religious observance; Tyson did not dare attempt it. "The Germans," he said, "appreciate Christmas, but are not familiar with our 'Thanksgiving.'" Undoubtedly he talked with Ebierbing and Tookoolito about the meaning of the day and perhaps of his family at home. Perhaps grace was said as they lifted their cans to their lips.

All the while the dark night ruffled itself over them like a giant bird on a nest—a black version of the Holy Ghost. Underneath, far below the ice, fingerless, one-eyed Sedna wept in her watery home because no one came to untangle and comb her hair. Her guard dog kept a wary eye on the door. There could be visitors at any time.

Chapter Six

*

November 29, 1872–December 25, 1872

Ice: Drifting Down the Country in the Pack

Members of the Polaris *ice raft* (back row, from left to right): *Captain Tyson, Tookoolito, Gustavus W. Lindquist, William Linderman, John Herron, John W. C. ("Robert") Kruger, Frederick Jamka, Frederick Meyer;* (middle row, left to right): *Ebierbing, Punny, Mersek, Succi, Augustina, Tobias, Hans, William Jackson;* (front row, left to right): *Peter Johnson and Frederick Aunting;* (not shown): *Charlie Polaris, infant child of Mersek and Hans.*

Polar ice affected coastal life in profound ways, from natural habitat to spiritual views. The people who lived on the edge of the ice, dependent on its animals for every aspect of their lives, also lived in constant danger. Variations in weather and availability of game threatened existence in every season. If the seals did not come, or the caribou, if a walrus could not be captured, a polar bear, or, at the least, ducks, a community might be wracked by starvation. The weak would be left behind while those who still could hunt moved on toward any possibility of prey.

Human life was seen as a cyclical process bound inextricably with the cycles of weather and animals. When a disabled relative was left behind—abandoned in an igloo or tent constructed for the purpose—it was not from callousness but from a need for preservation of the whole. A dying person was grateful for a new, clean house of ice in which to die. Death was part of life. It was treated not with emotionalism but with practicality. Three days of mourning were countenanced. Then, with the deceased safely in heaven, happily wandering from star to star, it was time for the bereaved to move on.

Hunting, traveling, and living on the ice held their own unique dangers. Being swept out to sea on ice was one of the common perils of the Inuit who hunted sea mammals at the edge of the frozen sea. Endless were the accounts of such adventures, some with surprising and happy endings; most with no ending at all.

Whalers referred to the ice-choked waters of Baffin Bay and Davis Strait as "the country." As soon as they started entering the country, they, too, experienced the dangers of being caught in the ice and carried away. But unlike the local inhabitants, they did not have the clothing nor the means of hunting that enabled the Inuit to survive such exigencies. Deprived of fresh marine mammal meat, they were harried by scurvy as well as frostbite. They were totally dependent on their ship—however small and frail—and what was carried inside it.

To lose the ship was to lose life. Rare was the European sailor who survived without it. Willem Barents, beset in the ice, survived the winter of 1596–97 in a hut on Novaya Zemlya but died in June shortly after he and his men set out for Holland in two small open boats. Twelve of the original company of seventeen reached home in October. In June 1611, after wintering in the enormous bay that bears his name, Henry Hudson's crew turned mutinous. They put Hudson—along with his young son John and seven mostly disabled crewmen—into a small boat with "a peece, and powder, and shot, and some pikes, an iron pot, with some meale, and other things," and cast them adrift. They were never seen or heard from again.

Sometimes the danger to an ice-locked ship was so great, it was abandoned, only to be reboarded, sometimes again and again. Such was the saga of the *Diana*, which came into the country in the summer of 1866. The *Diana* had returned to the Shetlands after a disastrous spring sealing voyage to Jan Mayen Island before setting out again in search of whales. Whaling proved no better, and soon the ship—the first steam-powered whaler out of

Hull, England—was trapped in the ice of Baffin Bay. With no escape to be found, her captain determined to "drift down the country in the pack." The ship had only two months' provisions on board.

Over and over, the situation seemed so dire, with icebergs pushing against the frail hull in raging storms, the captain ordered her abandoned; and, for some time, the men lived on the ice. It was not until March of 1867 that the leaking, battered ship, with its captain lying dead on the deck, was able to break out of the pack. By the time she limped into Lerwick in the Shetlands the next month, a dozen crew members were dead, piled up alongside the captain. The rest were decimated by starvation and scurvy. *The Edinburgh Scotsman* reported:

> *The sight which met the eyes of the people from the shore who first boarded her cannot well be told in prose. . . . Coleridge's "Ancient Mariner" might have sailed in such a ghastly ship—battered and ice-crushed, sails and cordage blown away, boats and spars cut up for fuel in the awful Arctic winter, the main deck a charnel-house not to be de-scribed. The miserable, scurvy-stricken, dysentery-worn men who looked over her bulwarks were a spectacle, once seen never to be forgotten.*

There is an extraordinary similarity between the harrowing experiences of the *Diana* and her crew and the story of the *Polaris* ice floe adventurers. The *Diana*'s travails occurred six years earlier in approximately the same area over approximately the same length of time. The difference was, the whaling crew always had its ship, while the *Polaris* ice floe party did not. Also, the *Diana*'s crew, unable to hunt successfully, were totally dependent on the ship's stores, which were deficient to the point that hunger and scurvy soon overtook the sailors. With two able hunters, the ice floe party suffered no scurvy and no ill health except for the general debilitation of hunger.

Being carried away with the ice was not the only peril of the northern waters. Being crushed in the midst of two or more opposing fields of ice in motion was another terrifying fate. At any moment a beset ship—or a drifting ice colony—could be "nipped" and stove in. The power was enormous, the sounds of crushing—especially in the dark—horrific. The only possible defense was gunpowder, but what were explosives and fire compared to millions of tons of ice?

Now, aboard the *Polaris* floe somewhere in the middle ice of Baffin Bay, it was November 30, 1872—six weeks after the Separation. A westerly wind had calmed. Twilight was a streak in the south sky at noon: a glimmering from 11:00 A.M. until 1:00 P.M. Hope was dimming, but still there were steps to be taken.

Tyson got Herron, Jackson, Johnson, and Lindquist to struggle with him over the floe to the old hut in order to retrieve the canvas, with which it had been constructed. This was given to Hans to line his igloo. Hans had been working hard for the men, as had Mersek. It seemed only fair that they should be able to line their hut as the men had been able to line theirs.

Tookoolito spent much time alone with Punny and Tyson in the igloo they shared. Ebierbing was out hunting, even when Hans was sick and could not go. Often Tyson was laid low with rheumatism, simply too cold to function. For Tookoolito, there was always something to do—cleaning the floor, smoothing the walls clear of condensation, scraping out the substitute lamp to find bits that might be edible, drying and trying to repair clothing, talking with Punny, in Inuktitut as well as in English, telling her stories, stories she undoubtedly remembered from long-ago winter nights.

Tyson spent what time he could writing. He had come away from the Terrible Night with a pencil and some small notebooks. But now he discovered that his supply of paper had been pilfered and he no longer had enough to write every day. With too few clothes to walk around in outside and no firearm, his situation was further constrained. Already most of the party was lying in bed most of the time—partly because there was nothing to do and partly because of the need to conserve calories. Keeping quiet and as warm as possible could prolong life—and was all that could be done.

Tyson's greatest difficulty and concern was an increasingly dangerous misperception growing among the "German" faction. These men believed that they were in fact close to the east side of Davis Strait—Greenland, not far from Disko, where help would be available.

On December 6, a clear night, Meyer was able to take an observation. He had come away from the ship with a sextant and ice-horizon and star chart. He took the declination and right ascension of Cassiopeia. But lacking a nautical almanac, he could not make corrections and could only approximate the latitude. He calculated the position at 74°4' north, 67°53' west—in the vicinity of Disko. It was what his men wanted to hear. There were the supplies the *Congress* had left behind, carefully preserved in a storehouse owned by the Danish government at Godhavn.

Tyson insisted they were nowhere near that far south. Meyer said the wind was blowing from the northwest, therefore pushing them to the east. Tyson maintained the heavy ice was not affected so much by wind as by current and that their drift was to the west, toward Baffin Island. Tyson had no navigational equipment but did have a tremendous amount of experience and ice savvy; he had spent years navigating through the arctic seas. He had gone where others had not dared. He had spent months beset and adrift in the country and survived storm, shipwreck, and near starvation. He knew the currents and what the ice was likely to do.

Nowhere does Tyson state that he consulted with Tookoolito or Ebierbing as to location, though he might well have. Inuit wayfinding was an essential part of life—as important as finding and killing animals. Indeed, it was a major part of hunting. It was a skill that developed from experiential knowledge and involved topography, geography, hydrography, weather, astronomy, place-names, animal behavior, and oral tradition. It was the literacy of survival.

The couple with whom Tyson found himself bound in the dark igloo had excellent references as wayfinders. Tookoolito's brother Eenoolooapik had first mapped Cumberland Sound and enabled the whalers to fish there, while Ebierbing served as a pilot for its difficult, ice-choked waters. Ebierbing had guided Captain Parker's *Truelove* through a narrow channel 128 miles long from Niantilik, in Cumberland Sound, to Cornelius Grinnell Bay. Tookoolito's other brother Totocatpik was renowned as a voyager, and she herself was brought up with a sharp awareness of her coastline. She had often served as tracker for Hall—out in front of the dogs, picking a way through hummocky ice.

Tyson feared that the men would bolt with the boat and the provisions, leaving him and the two Inuit families with almost no resources. This would mean death to all of them—those who left and those who stayed. Of equal concern was the thought that Tookoolito and Ebierbing might themselves bolt. Not only did they stand a chance of succeeding, they had reason to flee: fear of cannibalism. In early December, Ebierbing had given Tyson his pistol, saying, he didn't "like the look out of the men's eyes." Tyson stated further: "I know what he fears: *he thinks they will first kill and eat Hans and family, and then he knows Hannah's, Punny's, and his turn would be next.*"

Cannibalism, though not often mentioned in polite society and avoided in the nineteenth-century record, was a fact of life in the Arctic. When reports reached England that members of the Franklin party had eaten fallen fellows, the revulsion was so great that interest in the rescue search for them waned. Forensic evidence now indicates that it had been widely practiced as the starving men of the *Erebus* and *Terror* weakened and collapsed. In 1921, the Greenlandic-Danish ethnographer Knud Rasmussen recorded the following story of a woman named Ataguvtaluk in a time of famine. The speaker is Takornaoq, a native of the Igdlulik (Igloolik) people from Fury and Hecla Strait:

> *"I once met a woman who saved her own life by eating her husband and her children.*
>
> *"My husband and I were on a journey from Igdlulik to Ponds Inlet. On the way he had a dream; in which it seemed that a friend of his was being eaten by his own kin. Two days after, we came to a spot where strange sounds hovered in the air. At first we could not make out what it was, but coming nearer it was like the ghost of words; as if it were one trying to speak without a voice. And at last it said:*
>
> *"* 'I am one who can no longer live among humankind, for I have eaten my own kin.'
>
> *"We could hear now that it was a woman. And we looked at each other, and spoke in a whisper, fearing what might happen to us now. Then searching round, we found a little shelter built of snow and a fragment of caribou skin. Close by was a thing standing up; we thought at first it was a human being, but saw it was only a rifle stuck in the snow. But all this time the voice was muttering. And going nearer again we found a human head, with the flesh gnawed away. And at last, entering into the shelter, we found the woman seated on the floor. Her face was turned towards us and we saw that blood was trickling from the corners of her eyes; so greatly had she wept.*
>
> *"* 'Kikaq' (a gnawed bone), she said, 'I have eaten my husband and my children!'

"She was but skin and bone herself, and seemed to have no life in her. And she was almost naked, having eaten most of her clothing. My husband bent down over her, and she said:

" 'I have eaten him who was your comrade when he lived.'

"And my husband answered: 'You had the will to live, and so you are still alive.' . . ."

Rasmussen provides a photograph of the woman, which clearly shows discolored skin around her mouth. He notes: "Blue veins show up prominently round her mouth, said to be due to her having eaten her own flesh and blood."

Rasmussen's colleague Peter Freuchen married a woman from Thule with a grisly heritage. Navarana's grandfather had lost an eye in a fight with cannibals and watched as his mother was carried away to be eaten. When Navarana was a child living with her parents on Salve Island, writes Freuchen,

One of those inexplicable epidemics that so pitifully ravage a primitive race struck the people, and on the island where they lived only Navarana, her mother and her small brother were spared. They had no meat to eat and were forced to butcher their dogs for food. When this source of supply was exhausted they ate their clothes and dog traces and anything available. The little boy was about three years old and was still nursing. The mother soon had no milk left, and the child in a frenzy of hunger bit the nipple off her breast. Then, seeing no hope of keeping him alive, she hanged him while Navarana looked on. The mother's grief, Navarana told me, was worse than the sight of the dead child, and she swore to her mother that she did not want to die, no matter how hungry she was, but would remain to comfort her.

These stories are particularly striking because they come as late as fifty years *after* the ice drift—at a time when the white man's moral code was more dominant and at a time when news traveled further, sometimes even into print. How much more prevalent was cannibalism fifty years earlier?

In the high latitudes, hunger was just over the next ridge or curled up like a dog outside your door. It changed form, but its manifestations were always nightmarish. Cannibalism, infanticide, desertion: Here were the Three Horsemen of the Arctic Apocalypse.

Dark thoughts dwelled in Tookoolito's dark snow hut, as they did in the other two huts as well: Where might starvation lead them? No adult could keep from mentally calculating over and over the provisions and dividing by nineteen, or dreaming of long-ago feasts at home, especially during this, the season of the turning of the year. No child could keep from crying of hunger.

In the meantime, the cold intensified. During the second week of December, the temperature held at twenty-one or twenty-two degrees below zero. Tyson and Meyer seemed to suffer the most: Tyson with cold and rheumatism, and Meyer with an undisclosed ailment, undoubtedly a manifestation of malnutrition.

Hunger and cold exacerbated each other. But there were no cracks in the ice and no seals. Unless there are seals, there are usually no bears; and, without bears, usually no arctic foxes following behind in their tracks to pick at their kills. Linderman, however, did succeed in shooting a small fox—"all hair and tail," Herron commented. It provided a mouthful for each of seven men. Hans constructed an ice trap and caught one of the small white foxes as well. Hans also made a hole in the ice and set a seal net, to no avail.

The daily allowance was cut again. The pitiful rations of bread and canned meat were combined and mixed with brackish water for seasoning and warmed in a tin can over the lamp or fire. (As the men ran out of firewood from the boat, they gradually adapted to the lamp; finally, they had no choice but to learn how to use it.) The rations were the same for each in the three igloos, but pilfering was continuous. "We feel sometimes as though we could eat each other," Herron lamented.

In the mostly calm weather of mid-December, the scene was quiet, a frozen tableau. There was no sense of struggle. Tyson wished only that if he perished, some of his company would survive to tell the truth of the *Polaris*. For now, there was nothing to do but try to survive and to protect the two families. Until seals came, they had to wait—and drift, lieges of the current. Resignation wrapped the scene in its own quiet mantle. And discipline was entirely missing.

In the vicinity of the igloos, there was no regular activity—no prescribed period of exercise, no religious observance, no routine. Rarely did anyone venture outside and, if someone did, fleetingly, the figure could barely be made out in the darkness. When the hunters left for the edge of the floe, their shapes were quickly absorbed by their surroundings and lost behind the rugged ice. There was only occasional smoke and never a real light. No wild animals came near, no birds. If seen from afar, the floating hamlet was camouflaged—small white domes on the ice that might not be noticed except by a trained eye. If experienced as a movie, the background music would be adagio, transcribed for organ: slow and stately, suited to a crystal white progression of several degrees per month.

Sometimes, while the members of the group rested and tried to sleep, seals would swim beneath them, swishing through the dark waters searching for cracks in the ice. As their smooth, blood-filled, milk-rich bodies swirled and turned, small bubbles would rise and press against the frozen floor of the starving captives. On December 20, Ebierbing and Hans tried and failed to capture some of these hidden seals. Still, this was new hope. With the shortest day of the year passing, there was also thankfulness for the anticipated return of the sun. "Our spirits are up," Herron commented, "but the body weak." Thoughts turned to Christmas.

On the nights of December 23 and 24, with strong northerly winds blowing, brilliant auroras blazed across the sky. In the twilight of Christmas noon, the group ate breakfast: four ounces of bread and two-and-a-half ounces of pemmican warmed over the lamp. Some called the concoction "soup" and some called it "tea," but all were delighted with the extra ounce of bread that Tyson had allocated for the day. Dinner was far better: Each had a small piece of frozen ham, two whole biscuits, a few mouthfuls of dried apples, and a few swallows of seal's blood. It was the last of the ham, the last of the apples, and the last of the available seal's blood, but it was a Christmas feast to be relished and remembered.

With the feast over, Tyson went back out to the storehouse to see just what was left: nine cans of pemmican and six bags of bread. At the present rate, he calculated, the pemmican would last two months and the bread three. Possibly, by then, game would be available, but no whalers could be expected until April or May.

By evening, a strong wind that had been blowing for several days turned into a gale with heavy drifting snow. They were, Tyson figured, at a latitude of about 72°, in the middle of Baffin Bay. The land to the west, which he could just make out on the coast of Baffin Island, was, he estimated, forty or fifty miles away.

This country of ice that was no country was immense and impossible to understand. Its nature and terrain were defined by a wide vocabulary: Scoresby listed and described eighteen different types, or conditions, of ice, devoted ninety-seven pages to it, and brought back from his travels ninety-six careful drawings of arctic snowflakes. Still, the kingdom of ice recognized no laws of geography or physics. Even when you could read weather by interpreting the drift of snow, it was not enough. In a second, everything could be different, and you were lost.

Toward the west end of Davis Strait lay a land Tookoolito and Ebierbing knew as the "Dreaded Land"—a group of islands between Frobisher Bay and Cyrus Field Bay off the end of Hall Peninsula. It was also known as Lok's Land. Many of their people used to live there until a time long ago when nearly all of them were out together on the ice. The ice separated from the shore and carried them away. They never came back, nor did any Inuit ever hear of them again. The dread of the place was so great that no Inuit wanted to go there. It was a dread that had been passed from parent to child and could not be erased, as Ebierbing had once explained. Now the currents were carrying them there, to its source, taking them home to horror.

Chapter Seven

December 26, 1872–February 2, 1873

LIGHT RETURNS; THE LAST DOG DIES

This is dangerous work requiring a correction in course, but I have no tools. I am worse off than Meyer who had a sextant and ice-horizon but no nautical almanac. I am even worse off than Tyson, who had no equipment at all but depths of experience. I have neither, only an obsessive desire to find the truth.

How do I get inside the dark hut and illuminate Tookoolito? I have clues, hints, and the maddingly few words that Tyson provides. There he was with her, hour after long hour, month after dark month. He could have asked anything of her, but he gave us so little! Unlike Hall, he apparently never thought to question her about her life and beliefs—or can it be that paper was just too precious? Now, more than a century later, there is no one to interview. The chain of memory is broken; pieces hang like swinging filaments of a once perfect spider web. There is only the argument between fact as we know it—what Tyson wrote on the rationed sheets of his small notebooks—and what the heart longs for: a conversation with Tookoolito.

I want the power of the angakok to do the impossible, to reach the unreachable, to visit forbidden realms. I want time travel and the choice of parallel universes. I want to go back and sit beside her, to offer alternatives, and ask advice. Of course, to ask direct questions would be impolite, but I am sure she would be glad of conversation and more than willing to help.

I take comfort in the thought that I am on a different floe—close enough to be aware of the *Polaris* party but not so close that I can hear what is being said or see exactly what is happening. There is the wind, the snow, and the grinding and groaning of the ice. There is fog. Fog alters the apparent horizon and the angle of the sun, making it impossible to determine latitude. According to Scoresby, fogs also, by increasing the apparent distance of objects, "appear, sometimes, to magnify men into giants, hummocks of ice into mountains, and common pieces of drift-ice into heavy floes or bergs." Fogs, when freezing, can fall from the rigging and cut the hands or faces of those on deck.

Every so often the curtain of ice pulls back, and I can catch a glimpse. Once, while working at the Joint Institute for Laboratory Astrophysics in Boulder, Colorado, I edited a 1,000-page book of theoretical astrophysics. Still, I cannot grasp how we are made of stardust. Or how the universe is expanding ever outward, pulling us with it on our wobbling home, Earth; and to where? Is this our ice floe—a speck in the ocean of time and space propelled by explosion and carried outward by currents beyond our understanding? There are billions and billions of galaxies, and no two are alike, any more than any two snowflakes are alike. Is each galaxy, also, an ice floe being carried out into space?

What I see is this: At a precise moment 15 billion years ago, for some inexplicable reason, something detonated the "big bang"—an explosion that set the universe into being and motion, an explosion that lives in each cell of our bodies, tying us to that mysterious beginning and to one another. Now, at our birth and at each crisis or major turn in our lives, there is a smaller "big bang": Holograms of the universe, we set out on a new dark drift, as much wanderers as the planets, the stars, and their dust. We do not know *why* but only *is:* Something happened; here we are—in motion and alone, occasionally calling to one another across the black river.

On the night of October 15, 1872, in the far northern waters of Smith Sound, two icebergs pushed against the piece of ice to which the *Polaris* was moored and created a "big bang." Nineteen persons were set adrift on a floe—a new, small, wobbling planet with an unknown trajectory carrying its population out into the night.

Over and over, we are set adrift, clinging to whatever comes to hand, hoping the current will bring us out of danger to something we can call home. Once, we were all part of the same star. Now, blown apart as fragments, we are traveling out and out into an endless expansion through something called dark matter, which we do not understand. We catch a glimpse of one another here and there, ships locked in ice, but are quickly torn away.

In the nineteenth century, when ships met at sea and communicated with one another, they were said to "speak" one another: "In the afternoon we spoke the American ship *McLellan.* . . ." When conditions allowed, parties might board one another's ships. If family members were present, a rare opportunity for sociability and exchange of news ensued.

Once my husband Martin and I were on a rafting trip down the Colorado River. It was intensely hot. The guides in the different pontoon boats said, "There is a place coming up where you can jump out, into the river, and the current will carry you to shore." Suddenly, they said, "Now! If you're going, you have to jump NOW!" I did. What I saw, from the shock of the cold water, was all of us who had jumped spread out over a wide section of the river. My arms and legs were almost immediately paralyzed with the cold. I could barely move. The current was too strong to swim against in any regard. All I could do was float within my life jacket, hoping it would hold. We were being carried far apart, some out of sight, and around a huge bend in the river. Some started screaming, but there was no help. There was no one near me. Each of us was alone. The guides had been wrong, I decided. I had made a terrible mistake. Then I was getting close to shore—huge rocks—and waves were breaking over my head. I saw my two young children, presently in the care of my mother and father. I was going to survive and get back to them, I told myself. And I did. It was not my whole life that flashed in front of me but the part that made me need to live.

Physicists like to call the universe "elegant." The word ("graceful in appearance or manner") appears frequently in their writings—at least those for laypeople. What does it mean, when the universe is also an explosive, cannibalistic cauldron of creation with galaxy eating galaxy and each of us a swirl of dust without a place to hide?

From a distance, the tableaux of the *Polaris* ice floe could be seen as elegant—the stately and dignified procession of a regal barge, such as that carrying the corpse of King Arthur to Avalon, or that carrying a young and hopeful Queen Elizabeth down the Thames in celebration of her birthday.

But, inside the ice prison, there was nothing elegant. No matter how hard she worked, there was little Tookoolito could do. The blood of seals could not be removed from the floor or, when she menstruated, the blood from her body. Menstruating women were forbidden to have contact with hunters. They must stay by themselves and eat by themselves—and only what was permitted. The hands of menstruating women appear red to the animals of the sea, and a vapor rises from them, which is distasteful. Anyone who comes in contact with a bleeding woman gives rise to this vapor and frightens off the seals. Sedna becomes angry. A bleeding woman must announce herself and keep her distance. But what could Tookoolito do, or Mersek? How could they satisfy Sedna when they were trapped like this? An angakok would demand public confession. Once the transgressor had confessed, all would be forgiven. Sedna would release seals. But there was no angakok. And there was no Bible, either, or minister—no public form of prayer. How could she confess?

Conditions could only get worse. Tyson had been going over the provisions in the storehouse and calculating. Tookoolito had saved some dried seal skin for the repair of clothing, but now it must be eaten. She did what she could to warm it, but there was not enough blubber to cook and soften it, and Tyson could not manage it; his jaws became too sore.

Four days after Christmas, Hans shot a seal but lost it. Then Ebierbing got his chance. His seal floated away from him, but he called as loud as he could for his kyack. When several of the men got it to him, he went after his prey and secured it. There was meat again, but not much to go around. When a seal is properly divided, Tyson said, there is only one way to do it, and that is with openness and fairness.

First, the blood must be carefully preserved, passed around for each to drink a portion or saved for later use. The liver, heart, and brain, considered delicacies, are divided equally, as is the flesh. The eyes are given to the youngest child. The entrails are scraped and allowed to freeze for future use, and the skins are saved for clothing, or for making kyacks, tents, and the reins and harnesses for dogsleds.

New Year's Day 1873 brought the coldest temperature since the party had unwillingly set out two and one-half months before: twenty-nine degrees below zero. Dinner consisted of frozen entrails from Ebierbing's last small seal along with a little pemmican tea. There was nothing special—no commemoration by means of food or ritual. "A happy New-year for all the world but us poor, cold, half-starved wretches," Tyson commented. ". . . moldy bread and short allowance," Herron remarked.

Among Tookoolito's people, the return of the light at the beginning of the year was commemorated with a ritual: Two men would start out from their igloos, one dressed to represent a woman. They would go to every house in the village, blowing out the light in each. A new fire would then be started. Hall had once asked Tookoolito what this meant; she answered, "New sun—new light."

Now the twilight had stretched to six hours daily. She was definitely coming back—the sun woman who had been so wronged and yet was so faithful. According to Franz Boas, the ethnologist who interviewed natives of Cumberland Sound in 1883–84, the origin of the sun and moon is incest. Inuit legend has it that a woman was sexually abused by her disguised brother. When she discovered who her attacker was, she ran out of the house with a lighted stick, and he followed her with another lighted stick. As they ran around the house, the brother fell and his flame went out, while hers continued to burn brightly. They were wafted up to the sky, where she became the sun and he became the moon.

As the light was increasing, the provisions were shrinking. At the end of the first week of the year, there remained eight cans of pemmican and five bags of bread; Tyson estimated that these supplies would last two and one-half months. But they were disappearing faster than the distribution of rations would allow. The men, convinced they could soon break away to Disko, refused to acknowledge how vital these provisions were. Thinking their time on the floe was short, they were helping themselves—and building up strength for their trip. A guard posted at the supply house was an impossibility. No one in such circumstances could be expected to stand watch. It was now—as of January 9—thirty-six degrees below zero at noon. And so, on the ice island that had floated beyond law, there was no punishment attempted for transgressions that might otherwise have led to floggings or worse.

Then, the temperature dipped even further, to thirty-seven degrees below zero. On January 12, Tyson went seeking a bag of clothes that had been thrown overboard on the Terrible Night—shirts and drawers, a pair of pants, a vest, as well as several pairs of stockings—which he had been saving for a time when there were no huts and they would be traveling over the ice. The bag was gone. Robbed again, Tyson had to continue half clad, with no coat or long pants, only short breeches. "All my little additional store, which I had relied on for traveling, has been stolen," he lamented. "It was very little, but I needed it so much . . . and now, when they have made up their minds to travel, without consulting me, they have robbed me of everything."

The ice to westward was solid, denying the opportunities for seals. So much had been stolen, Tyson figured, the party might have to try for land even though they could not reach it. Either way, as he saw it, theirs would be a "struggle for life."

January 13, the temperature dropped to forty degrees below zero. Two days later, it began to snow and blow heavily with the temperature rising to fourteen degrees above zero. By the sixteenth, there was a real change: after relative silence, the sound of ice, pushing and groaning. This meant cracks, bringing seals. It also meant the destruction of the party's floating home and the loss of what little stability they had known.

Suddenly, there came the glorious cry: "Kyack!"

Tyson rounded up some of the men and got them to help carry the remaining kyack a mile to the edge of the floe. It was a struggle because of their weakness and the hummocks they had to cross, but they were in time. Hans and Ebierbing secured the seal they had shot, and the party returned to their snow huts in triumph.

But when Tyson ordered the seal to be taken to Ebierbing's igloo, Kruger forced it into the men's igloo instead. There it was divided to the men's satisfaction, not as custom dictated and certainly not in the spirit of community and communion, which was expected. The hunters were given only a small portion of the meat and a little blubber. Increased fear for survival was their only reward. "He [Kruger] is head thief and head mutineer," Tyson wrote in his field book.

The remaining two dogs came in limping, apparently after a skirmish with a bear. The compact world of the ice floe was opening up to the stream of life—seals, which meant bears, which meant foxes, which meant birds. All of which meant food.

Tobias, the six-year-old son of Mersek and Hans, was sick. It was January 17, and the temperature had dropped sharply to thirty-eight degrees below zero, with a strong wind blowing. The daily rations were now cut again, leaving not nearly enough calories to protect against the cold. Both hunters said that, although they had often suffered periods of hunger, they had never known anything like the present conditions. In spite of the fact that they were outside, moving vigorously, they had the same rations as the men who lay about in their igloo, sleeping and playing cards. Tyson dared not adjust the rations in favor of the hunters. Doing so, he said:

> . . . would cause open mutiny among the men; and such harmony as can be preserved I am bound to maintain, for the good of all. Notwithstanding all my discomforts, my dark and dirty shelter, my bed of wet and musty musk-ox skins, fireless and cheerless and hungry, without one companion who appreciates the situation, I shall be well content, and even happy, if I can keep this party—worthy and worthless—all altogether without loss of life until April, when I hope for deliverance.

January 19, a longed-for event occurred: The sun returned after an absence of eighty-three days. And, with the sun came a seal, to bring light and warmth into the huts. Soon after, bears and dovekies were spotted, though there was no land visible. The birds, the first noted, must have brought a surge of hope and wonder. Smallest of the alcids, they are known today as little auks. Similar to starlings and with wings that whir, they return in spring to their crowded breeding sites on far northern cliffs. To northern whalers, and especially to those who were trapped in the ice, they were analogous to Noah's dove.

A well-known song of the time in the Cumberland Sound area has a refrain that, translated literally, goes: "Northward, northward! I am inclined to walk the sky to its hole, the birds to their country." Tookoolito must have heard this song and known it as a child. Perhaps it echoed in her memory as the birds were sighted.

According to Tyson, the ice floe party was in the middle of the strait, at about latitude 70° north. Meyer agreed with the latitude but continued to insist that they were close to Disko. The men, emboldened by his assertiveness, were ready to revolt, and the tension in the camp broke with stunning speed. On January 24, Kruger burst into the igloo that Tyson shared with Tookoolito and her family, taunting and threatening the man who, he perceived, stood between him and freedom. Tyson refused to respond. Kruger retreated, then returned later to apologize. There was no knowing how many backers he had in the men's hut or whether Meyer had sent him to test Tyson. Of Myer, Tyson commented, "They believe that he is a German Count."

The next afternoon, a large seal brought home by the hunters further subdued the scene. For Tyson and his housemates there was a dinner of raw liver, about a yard of seal's entrails, pemmican tea, and, for dessert, a little blood and blubber: a meal to be noted and remembered. Tyson still had his pipe and a little tobacco—an extraordinary luxury.

After the feast, there was more grumbling from the men, but Tyson, as he explained, had reasserted his authority over division of seal meat. He had taken to bringing newly caught seals into Ebierbing's hut and dividing them equally among the men, the Inuit families, and himself. The men, grown tired of the labor of skinning a frozen seal, had relinquished their authority; they did not even accept Tyson's invitation to send witnesses to the butchering.

Cold at forty degrees below zero continued, with the hunters trying to reach the water they thought they saw to the east. On January 25, one of the two remaining dogs disappeared. Ebierbing and Hans had each taken one along on their difficult and separate treks to the eastern edge of the floe. Hans let his out of the harness, and the dog bolted. Tyson claimed it was their best bear-dog and bitterly blamed Hans for its loss.

By the morning of January 26, the temperature had fallen to forty-two degrees below zero, the coldest temperature so far. A brilliant aurora lit the sky. The brightest of these tend to appear in the coldest weather. They also come in cycles of 11 years. Reports further indicate that activity swells in wider cycles of 80 years and 250 years. Historic sightings over large areas of earth were recorded in the early seventeenth century. Between 1645 and 1715, the aurora was little seen; then a great display broke the darkness in 1716, and again in 1722. In the nineteenth century, auroral displays peaked in 1870. During the winter of the *Polaris* ice floe drift, they were in ebb. Tyson does not often mention displays and, when he does, it is with restraint. Because he was inside most of the time, he undoubtedly missed some bursts; and, he had but the one pencil and a dwindling supply of paper. There were more pressing subjects on his mind.

Indigenous people had been trying to make sense of auroras long before foreigners entered their realm. In nearly all northern cultures, the phenomenon is associated with the afterlife and is generally considered beneficent. It is also often seen as a source of power, one that can be called down.

Today we know that electrons and protons flowing from the sun on the solar wind hit atoms and molecules of oxygen and nitrogen in earth's atmosphere, resulting in photons, or tiny flashes of light, which lead to the waving curtains of color that constitute the aurora. But we do not understand the exact workings of the solar wind or the sun and their relationship with earth.

When I lived in Alaska, I would sometimes stand in the middle of our intersection on a bitterly cold night looking up at the sky in wonder. Sometimes groups would be standing out on sidewalks and street corners looking upward, trying to block city lights from their view. Even when it was very late, I might wake my children for the event and have them look through the upstairs window to the north. I heard the noises, too. They are much disputed and have never been recorded. But I heard them—a crackling. The aurora has a voice.

That afternoon of January 26, 1873, the day of the coldest temperature, Ebierbing brought home a seal—a large one—that came as a welcome surprise to his housemates, who had just finished a meal of pemmican tea. It was particularly welcome to Tyson, who was on his last plug of tobacco. By night, the mercury in their thermometer had frozen—there was no telling how cold it was—and it stayed frozen the next day.

There was seal-blood soup but still not enough meat for more than two meals a day. Now that the light came so early and lasted so long, the hours stretched out between breakfast and dinner even more interminably. At one in the afternoon on the day of January 27, the hunters came home:

The weather was too severe even for them. The next day was only slightly warmer, and Ebierbing and Hans went out to try again.

Inside the huts, the argument continued as to where they were. Tyson knew that dioptrics, or the study of refraction, must be considered. The island of Disko, he maintained, with its high, rocky coastline, could be seen 80 miles away. Raised by refraction, it could be seen 100 miles away. Refraction, that optical magician of the Arctic, could bring what was distant close and magnify it to gargantuan proportions or turn it upside down. An owl could easily become a polar bear and cause great consternation. A mountain or an iceberg could become a castle with battlements; extraordinary images could float inverted in the sky. Clearly, Disko was not there or they would see it.

But no arguments could suffice. Tyson simply hoped to keep the men from leaving too soon. If only they would wait, there would be cracks in the ice, and seals. Then, too, there might be rescue. Tyson remembered the runaways from the *Ansel Gibbs* and the stories of the *Truelove*. He remembered, too, when Captain Hall rescued him from the *Georgiana* during the gale in Cyrus Field Bay in September 1860, and his narrow escapes with the *Era* caught in the ice at Niantilik Harbor in 1867 and 1869–70. On board the *George Henry* with Captain James Budington, he had found and helped save the *Resolute*. And when the *George Henry* went down, all the crew survived, as did Captain Quayle and the crew of the *McLellan*. Stories of rescue, coincidence, and crossed paths were countless; he himself was part of the literature of amazing escape. Rescue was not too much to hope for, especially since they were moving so rapidly south toward the whalers.

But even now, with the miles flowing by and the light opening like a giant polynya (area of open water) in the sky, the hunters were out at their work, and the igloo-bound had only seal skin to eat. There was not enough fuel to cook it, but only to warm it—hair and all.

The hunters returned empty-handed at 6:00 in the evening. The last dog had become sick and died on its way back to camp with Ebierbing. Tyson feared it was the well-picked bones he had given the dog the night before. This was the first natural death of the entire group. The difference between men and beasts, Tyson noted, must be *hope*. The dogs could not look ahead to any possible relief; they could not anticipate a change in their miserable situation as the people were still able to do.

It was remarkable what these dogs accomplished and the role they played in everyday life as well as in the exploration of the Arctic. Like their native drivers, they have seldom been acknowledged. Chroniclers for the most part simply did not consider dogs and their individual contributions significant. Hall, by contrast, noted them in a number of instances, starting with his visit to Holsteinborg, Greenland, when heading north on his first voyage. From then on, he listed and commented on them, leaving a scattering of dog anecdotes throughout his journals.

Soon after they sailed from Greenland, one of his dogs, Barbekark, distinguished himself by playing a trick on his master. Hall was feeding the dogs, in a circle around him. He would throw each in turn a small dried fish until each dog had received a total of ten. Barbekark, quickly assessing the system of distribution, would back out of his position as soon as he had gotten a fish and push his way back into the circle further along in order to receive twice what the other dogs were getting. Flushed with success, and reading his master's smile as approbation, he then speeded up to a second move per round, thus getting three fish for every one the other dogs were getting. This sagacious dog became Hall's constant companion until Barbekark died in the United States between the first and second expeditions. On at least one occasion, Barbekark saved Hall's life—reviving him and leading him to safety when he was caught out in a ferocious storm while on a rescue mission. On another occasion, he saved the life of First Mate Rogers of the *George Henry* and an Inuit traveling companion when they became lost in blinding snow. He further distinguished himself by once hunting down a caribou.

Famished dogs would attack a sledge or rush into an igloo and grab whatever they might swallow. Sometimes, when starving, they would have to have their mouths tied to keep them from eating the trace lines of the harness as they ran. They were a constant danger and annoyance, fighting, howling, and causing trouble. They could wheel around, while running, and overcome the driver. They could tangle the lines and, while being sorted out, could drag their masters some distance. Hall's predecessor, Kane, complained of how they attacked his specimens on deck, even eating birds' nests—feathers, filth, and all. Danish explorer Peter Freuchen later commented on how dogs completed the cycle of human elimination:

When they [the Inuit] leave the igloo to continue their voyage, the last thing the travelers do is to relieve themselves. . . .

This is due to one peculiarity about the Eskimo dogs: they love human excrement more than anything else in this world. Out in the open, distressing situations can therefore arise. The process has to be done quickly, because of the cold, but the dogs crowding around can make it even more difficult. If there are other people in the party, somebody will take position in front of the suffering one and keep the dogs at bay with a whip.

But while the igloo is available, everybody takes advantage of it. Afterward, of course, the always hungry dogs are let in so that they can do away with the garbage and other things they can find.

Dogs would often escape and stray, causing many precious calories as well as hours to be lost in their recapture. They would tear apart graves and eat the dead or, if they came upon it, an abandoned baby. They would eat one another. Sometimes a mother dog would roll on and suffocate a puppy and, when she could not lick it back to life, swallow it. Freuchen tells the story of how a bitch of his whelped in harness while traveling. He could neither stop for her nor put her on the sledge. As the pups dropped from her, the other dogs gobbled them up until, finally, with the ninth and last pup, she "whirled around and devoured it herself."

Their viciousness and tendency toward cannibalism aside—the result of chronic, ravenous hunger—these dogs would pull hundreds of pounds through conditions unimaginably rigorous on almost no food. The camels of the north, in good times, they would be fed two or three times a week; in bad times, once. Summers, they could be on their own. As Captain Penny discovered when he got to Cumberland Sound in the summer of 1857 and found himself surrounded by a pack of 200, it was common for the Inuit owners to leave their dogs unattended on an island to subsist as best they could until it was time to round them up for winter use. Sometimes the dogs would leave a track of blood as they traveled in harness, their paws cut by rough ice. The eighteen-foot-long whip used by drivers spurred them to extraordinary feats. In March 1869, as Hall started out for King William's Land, he calculated that his eighteen dogs were pulling an average of 292 pounds each.

The dogs were in constant peril—of storm, wolf, a bear's paw, a musk ox's hoof, a crack in the ice, a fight within the pack, frostbite of an extended penis, or a sharp bone swallowed. Even their color could be a danger. Tookoolito remarked that red dogs, thought to attract lightning, were killed at birth. Sometimes dogs would fall into wolf traps and be impaled on the spear at the bottom. Sometimes distemper and famine would strike simultaneously—a lethal conjunction for any settlement.

Working dogs would track and grab seals and enable their masters to bring down polar bears, walrus, and musk oxen. In life, their bodies would provide warmth for those who otherwise might perish of cold, and, in death, their skins were turned into clothes and bedding. They could find their way through storms, slosh their way through soft snow, and pick their way across hummocky ice floes breaking apart; they knew where the edge was—and how to get home. In extremity, the dogs became food. And all with little in the way of kind treatment by those they served. Whips, oars, hatchets, rocks, rifles—whatever came to hand—might be used to club them and keep order among them, especially at feeding time.

So important were dogs to the Inuit that they figured profoundly in myths of origin, such as in a story from Cumberland Sound that Franz Boas recorded, "The Woman Who Married the Dog." In this tale, a man at Padli had a daughter who refused to marry. Finally her father grew angry and told her to marry his dog. The following night a man came into the hut who wore trousers of red dog skin. He slept with the daughter, then dragged her away the next morning, only to reappear with her later. Every night the same man dressed in dog skin appeared and slept with the young woman. Eventually, the woman had a litter of pups, and the father took the young woman, the pups, and the dog to a small island. The father supplied seal meat for the pups until the young woman decided to take revenge: She had the pups kill her father. She then made a small boat and put some of her pups aboard to sail out into the world to find a living. Others she sent inland to become caribou hunters. While those who scattered became the other peoples of the world, the last of the brood who stayed with her became the ancestors of the Inuit.

According to Boas, both Sedna, the Inuit deity, and also the man in the moon own a dog. The man in the moon's dog is called Tirie'tiang and is dappled white and red. He pulls the sledge of the man in the moon who helps orphans and the poor. Dogs also have a presence in some of the most important Inuit rituals, such as the autumn festival observed to appease the wrath of Sedna and of any souls offended by the transgression of taboos. As practiced by the Nugumiut of Frobisher Bay, among whom Hall and Tookoolito and Ebierbing lived during the first expedition, one of the three principal masked characters has his face covered with dog skin. He represents *Noonagekshown*, a being who brings good health, fair weather, and abundant food. He also distributes women among the men.

As seals were the link between water and land, so dogs were the link between and among settlements. They made not only hunting possible; they made human contact possible—a contact that often made the difference between life and death. The Inuit knew their dogs had to be able to exist—and work—on little food. They did not withhold food out of cruelty any more than they entombed their dying—or, on occasion, killed their infants—out of cruelty. The Arctic made its demands.

Now, for the ice floe party, there were no more dogs, and a sense of even greater aloneness and desolation must have settled upon them. Dogs were part of the fabric of everyday life—constant companions in the struggle to survive. To not have dogs was to live impoverished and in acute danger, that much closer to the edge of the always-close abyss. To not have dogs was to live isolated and to die.

The floe moved on, ever more quiet and sepulchral. From a great distance, no real change would have been noted, much less the absence of a dog, rising from its snow nest and shaking itself. This small frozen world was continuing quietly on its inevitable but uncharted course to the south. From a plane, from a satellite, it would have appeared as a fleck of ice in a river of ice.

Terbouetie, dogs. May the currents be kinder to you in death than in life. May you run through the stars for joy—not for hunger. May you lie down in warmth and rest in contentment. May you hear what you never did before: Good job, dogs. Good dogs.

Ebierbing alone stood between the prisoners and death by starvation. Hans's child Tobias was still ill, and Tyson did not know what to do. The child's distended stomach could not manage pemmican. He wanted seal meat, but there was only dry bread to give him. The mercury remained frozen, and the men seldom came out of their igloos. Crouched inside, they had nothing to do but try to keep from freezing. There was almost nothing for diversion except for cards, which the men had crafted from some thick paper. Euchre was their game. Tookoolito and Ebierbing had made a checkerboard out of a piece of canvas, with the squares marked by Tyson's pencil and with buttons for "men." Punny dug with a knife into the snow wall of the igloo.

On January 29, Tyson noted:

> . . . It is now one hundred and seven days since I have seen printed words! *What a treat a bundle of old papers would be! All the world over, I suppose some people are wasting and destroying what would make others feel rich indeed.*

I remember visiting the Yupik village of Aleknagik near Dillingham, Alaska, where a teacher claimed to have read 103 books during one winter there. The specificity grabbed my heart as I looked through the tall, fading grasses of late summer at dogs barking from the roofs of their small houses. Beyond stretched the immensity of the lakes and mountains of the Kuskokwim. This teacher did not say "about one hundred books." She did not say "many" books. She said "103." Tyson said "107 days." Loneliness can wear this suit of numbers, a clothing as stark and unadorned as arithmetic.

On that day, Ebierbing returned early, empty-handed. He was very hungry. He and Tyson shared a meal of frozen seal's entrails with a little blubber.

The next day, Tyson wrote a sort of last will and testament. But what is printed in his book is a faint shadow of what he wrote by pencil in one of the small notebooks in his ice hut. He had come to the end of his strength and patience and had to set the record straight:

> *Now as death is liable to all men and especially to one in my situation I whish (sic) here to make a few remarks which whether I live or die I sincerely hope will come to light. I here brand Sailing Master and Ice Pilot Sydney O. Budington as a villain, a liar a thief a coward and a drunkard and now has I fear added murder to his many crimes.*

For ten closely written pages, Tyson vehemently sets forth his case. Budington, he claims, continually slandered Hall before and after his death, continually stole liquor, clothing, and the best provisions, which he arranged to be privately prepared in the galley by the cook, who was "a great favorite of his." Budington appropriated all of Hall's private property and papers and tried to get the "two Esquimaux" to assist in stealing from Hall. He proposed that the expedition return in the summer following Hall's death and, according to Tyson, stated, "I came for Green Backs Dam the north Pole. I fear we will never get out of this scrape Hall got us in this scrape he is dead and in hell I hope and I hope some of the rest will be there before long." Budington, Tyson declares, suggested scuttling the *Polaris* on the reefs near Upernavik and making their way down to Disko, claiming full government pay for the trip. Even more damning, Budington had predicted, a few days before Hall left on his last sledge trip, the commander's death: ". . . the dam old son of a bitch will die soon. . . ." Then, after Hall's death, Budington claimed the doctor had poisoned the commander. Tyson concludes:

> . . . *I have told Joe and Hannah, should anything happen to me, to save these books and carry them home. Their is some bad spelling as it is writen in the dark hut and with very cold finggers. . . . I swear before God that what is written here to be the truth. . . .*

No other statement related to the *Polaris* cries out as this does. Tyson, in extremity, had no lifeline left but the truth. If, indeed, Tyson's truth approaches objective reality and is not a mirage of desperation, Budington is indeed the culprit, the dark god of this world of woe. Tyson's outcry might be excused as delusion, except for what he wrote later, in his handwritten autobiographical statement. There, he reiterates every charge—and goes further. Interestingly, he adds to the sketch of William Jackson. Budington got him appointed cook in New London, Tyson claims, after getting all other cooks who had shipped discharged. This one, "after his own heart," Tyson said, "would lick hell out of the Steward if he said anything. . . ."

Tyson's explosion remained locked in graphite. On the surface, all remained quiet. The moon changed but little else. Calm, cold weather kept the ice smooth and solid as marble. There was general understanding, now, though both coasts were shrouded in fog, that Disko had been passed and left behind. The men, for the time being, appeared disappointed but resigned to have lost their promised land. Tyson was increasingly worried. Within weeks, he knew, the party would face the inevitable breakup of their floe.

Inside Tyson's igloo, little Punny, sitting wrapped in a musk ox skin, would say to her mother every few minutes, "I am *so* hungry." Tookoolito would go on with her work. If it was time for a meal, she would be pounding up biscuit into a fine powder. She would melt brackish ice in an old pemmican can cut in half and placed over the lamp, then put in the powdered biscuit and the daily ration of pemmican, warm the mixture, and serve it as "tea." If there was seal skin and blubber enough for the lamp, she would cook the skin, attempting to make it palatable for Tyson. To heat five quarts of water would require two or three hours. When the pemmican can used for cooking became perforated with use, she managed to plug the holes; Tyson never figured out how. She would do her best to keep her husband's clothes dry and their ice house clean, though personal cleanliness had been abandoned long before.

The rations, on February 2, were down to three bags of bread—about 400 pounds—and a little over five cans of pemmican, each weighing 45 pounds. It was the time of coldest weather and fewest seals. Sedna was locked away beneath them in her house of stone and whale bone, her dog guarding the door, her father deep in the shadows. There was no way to reach her, no way to confess. Her hair was uncombed, and her anger had turned to ice.

Chapter Eight

Hall's igloo at Noo-Wook

If you want to find what Charles Francis Hall had to say about Tookoolito, you must go to the Archives Center on the third floor of the National Museum of American History at the Smithsonian Institution in Washington, D.C.—the largest museum and research center in the world. You need an appointment. You must be let in through a locked glass door, show identification, sign a register, and fill out papers. You are then led into a room for researchers—two long metal tables with swivel chairs monitored by an eight-screen television console. You are shown an introductory video. When

the orientation is accomplished, you wait until the collection you have requested is wheeled in on a cart. It is housed in boxes. In the case of Charles
Francis Hall, eleven black archival boxes. You are to take only one box to
your table at a time and remove only one folder from the box at a time. On
a form, you list what boxes you work with, one by one, and initial them as
you put the boxes back on the cart.

I was in a hurry. I was also tired, after flying all night. I had one-and-a-half
days to find what I was looking for: the details of how Tookoolito and
Ebierbing adopted Punny. I knew the approximate date: between the death
of Tookoolito's second infant, Little King William, on May 13, 1866, and
their departure with Hall for King William's Land on March 23, 1869.

I wanted to find what no one had been able to tell me: just what efforts
Hall had gone to in order to secure for Tookoolito what she wanted more
than anything else, a child. I wanted to believe he had accomplished the task
soon after the baby's death, sometime in the summer of 1866. From study-
ing a description of the contents of the boxes ahead of time, I knew what I
wanted: Box 10. With a mix of awe and excitement, feeling both unworthy
of the task and anxious to get through it, I claimed the box, took it to the
table where I would be working, and opened it up. I took out the first folder:
.094, "Rough notes and journal entries, 1866."

Here were small hard-covered notebooks measuring about five inches
square and some field books containing small scraps of paper with closely
written notes. The pages were brittle and often watermarked and stained,
the writing crowded, the ink dried to a light sepia. (According to Craig Orr,
Assistant Manuscripts Archivist, who is responsible for the Hall collection,
nineteenth-century ink had a high iron gall content, which causes it to fade
over time.) Many pages were crossed out, the information transferred, I
gathered, to larger, more formal journals. Nothing that I wanted. I hurried on
to the next folder, and the next, and the next. There, at .097, I stopped. In
one of twenty-one small notebooks dealing with the sledge trip of April to
June 1866, I found written on May 13: "Now 1-30 p.m. and a terrible House
of mourning have we: 'Little King William' is dead. Was taken to its eternal
home—to the bosom of Jesus who loved little children—at 1:25 p.m. . . ."
And, after the burial, "We arrive back to our encampment bemoaning the
loss of the idol of our hearts." There—the words of Hall just as he put them
down, just as the event was happening in bitter cold and sorrow. In spite of

all his limitations, Hall had been a man of compassion who cared deeply about those he considered his friends.

Now, where was the adoption? Where was his description of how he had worked to heal the suffering of the best companion he ever had? Where was the heroic effort to plug the abyss in the heart of Tookoolito? Emboldened, I went on, small notebook after small notebook, scrap after scrap, lists, maps, observations, calculations, figures, columns, scratch marks, x's, all the cramped, cold, faded, washed-out motion of freezing hands in a hurry far more desperate than mine. Where? I was running out of time. Could I find it? Would I fail? Was I really not up to the task? Then, Box 7—.065—"Journal kept by Hall, Aug. 1866 to Sept. 1869." This was a large journal, like a ledger book, with a heavy, embossed leather cover, clearly a more formal housing for notes out of the small field notebooks. The handwriting had shrunk, and the ink had faded to the point where it was in some places almost impossible to read. I took out the small magnifying glass I had brought with me.

Skimming quickly, I went on to .066—"Private journal kept by Hall, Aug. 1866 to Sept. 1869." And then, August 22, 1866:

> . . . *For several weeks just passed, Ebierbing and Tookoolito have been wanting to take the infant child of Armou and adopt it as their own. Armou and his wife are very anxious they should do so but I strenuously object to it on the ground that I will not have children or babies again on such a sledge journey as the one undertaken last spring by myself and party (when Little King William died). . . . My mind is fixed on this point that Ebierbing and Tookoolito shall not adopt any bodies baby till after my journey to King Williams Land has been made. . . .*

Stunned, I stopped. He had not wanted Tookoolito to have a baby after all. His trip—his obsession—had to come first. Tukeliketa had died on the lecture circuit in the United States, Little King William on an attempt to reach the place for which he had been named. It was always King William's Land. It was always the lost Franklin men. It was always an insane fantasy that Hall would rescue survivors from the greatest disappearance of all times and achieve heroic proportions in the process.

A considerate employee, seeing me (one is well watched) struggling with my small magnifying glass, offered and brought me a large one, which opened up an entirely new vista. Suddenly, I was looking down, as if from a hilltop—an explorer surveying a sepia land of no table of contents, index, glossary, or directions of any kind: a land outside the atlas of the known. Snow and ice had melted into this ground and time had blown harshly across it; its features were wearing away. I tried the magnifying glass this way and that, as if flying over the terrain at different angles and speeds in a circling, dipping plane. I began to experience motion sickness. But there was treasure here: Tookoolito, hidden in these faint brown topographic ridges. Every so often there would be a glimpse, a hint, like a notch in a tree limb or a slight indentation, and I would rush off in pursuit:

> *Wednesday, Jan. 9, 1867, Ship's Harbor Island, Repulse Bay: Tookoolito is hard at work day after day making reindeer fur [dresses] for ourselves & the four men I am to hire. Never did I see a more busy body than Tookoolito. She works from early in the morning to 9 o'clock & oftimes 11:00. . . . This severe labor has been continued from some time previous to leaving our [encampment] near Ft. Hope to now. Surely for her <u>faithfulness in every respect</u> to this last Expedition . . . she deserves a rich reward & if my will or purpose can have it so, she will not be without what she deserves.*

But already it is almost a year since the death of Little King William and there is no baby adopted. What she wants is a baby. Captain Hall, be merciful. Let her have a baby.

As I turn the pages, I come across occasional detritus—or is it memorabilia?—a flower pressed and bleeding into the paper; a hair. There are also terrible, terrifying gaps in Hall's journals—*terra incognitas* and *meta incognitas* of despair bridged only, at best, by notes, sometimes on scraps of paper. Sometimes the daily accounts kept in field books are transferred to the ledger books, sometimes not. The narrative skips and backtracks. Separate accounts are also kept for matters pertaining to the Franklin search.

In Box 11 are thirty-eight field books describing a second trip to Igloolik from February 17, 1868, to June 28, 1868. They say nothing of Punny.

In the ledger books, the first reference I find to the adopted child Punny comes on Thursday, July 16, 1868,: "At midnight this party consisting of Jo (*sic*), Hannah, and her little one. . . ." Punny is not yet named, and her parents have become Joe (or Jo) and Hannah.

When the account picks up on August 21, 1868, it is in two columns of particularly constricted writing that is almost illegible. No magnifying glass can probe the depths of regret—this territory of despondency where all trails lead inward. Here, there is a literal and clear split, something like the break in a sheet of ice. There had, indeed, been a terrible fissure—the long, painful death of Patrick Coleman.

On October 3, 1868, Hall complains that he missed a deer because a little girl in the party was crying.

October 7, at the bottom of a large ledger page devoted to hunting, and almost indecipherable, he notes: " 'My Joe' & Hannah's little one upset coffee kettle this a.m.—got seriously scalded."

The ledger book goes blank until the turn of the year. January 22, 1869, Hall provides a vignette of Tookoolito learning to spell "baby." February 13, with the temperature at forty-eight degrees below zero, he gives an account of how a baby froze to death in bed when it rolled away from its mother— its adopted mother. The real mother, as Hall notes, gave it away because her two earlier babies had died young, "& to save the life of this last, she gave it away . . . but could not save her idol."

The leather-bound ledger book again goes blank, from February 28 to June 21, 1869. (It was during this time that Hall finally made his short dash to King William's Land, his notes made in small field books.) On July 3, 1869, he mentions "little Punny" by name—the first instance I find.

It would take numerous trips to the black boxes locked in the vaults of the Smithsonian before I could put together the scattered pieces of Punny's story. Very simply, it is this:

During the spring of 1868, on his return from his second trip to Igloolik (this time accompanied by Tookoolito and Ebierbing), Hall fell in with Punny's parents at North Ooglit Island. Her mother was Ooshoo, daughter of Takkeelikeeta, whose portrait George Lyon drew for William Edward Parry's narrative of his second voyage for the discovery of the Northwest Passage from 1821–23. Her father was Toogoolat. Ooshoo was able to tell Hall stories of white men who might have been with Franklin. Hall, taken with her intelligence and good memory, carefully recorded her history on the inside cover of his leather-bound "Sir John Franklin Book." During this period of Hall's conversations with Ooshoo, Tookoolito and Ebierbing adopted Punny. Several months later, Toogoolat took another wife and, with his remaining children, deserted Ooshoo, who traveled alone, almost starving to death, to take refuge with Hall and his Inuit companions near Repulse Bay. Tookoolito wanted to take Ooshoo back to the United States with them on board the *Ansel Gibbs*, and Hall assented, but it never happened. She became wife to Nukherzoo, one of Hall's group, and took part in the hurried expedition to King William's Land. Of Nukerzhoo, what we know is not promising. He once attempted to rape Tookoolito—part of a wife-exchange deal with Ebierbing, he claimed. And as we last see him, at the conclusion of the trek to King William's Land, he is stealing a young woman from a hostile tribe. What became of Ooshoo, so unlucky in husbands, we do not know, nor of Punny's siblings scattered like snow across the Melville Peninsula.

At the long research table, I was still struggling to find the pieces. At ten minutes before five on this particular Friday in June, the employee at the front desk was anxious to close down. Reluctantly, I shut the ledger book, put it back in its folder, the folder back in the box, the box back on the wheeling cart. In minutes, I was in a cab, headed for Union Station and a train to New York. I was going to make another visit to my mother.

My mother clings to the floe of the old and the broken. I go to visit her when I can, leaping from my floe to hers; the last time had been six weeks earlier. She would not remember I had been there then. She would not remember where I had come from or how.

Soon I was settled on the train, in a car containing a Christian youth group from Kansas on their way to the big city for four days of Broadway shows, including *Jesus Christ Superstar*, the U.N., and seminars on how to bring Christ into everyday life. With noise and sparks of energy bursting through the car and into other cars, they hurtled toward their future. How could I tell them: Look, it is dark outside, and each lighted window we are passing, we are passing forever. We live in a terrible house of mourning. It is made of dark matter, and it carries us into darkness. How could I tell them this? They were sweet. One volunteered to carry away my trash.

My mother lives in a small, pleasant co-op in the Carnegie Hill section of

Manhattan, one of the more desirable neighborhoods in New York. She woke up as I came in and got out of bed to greet me and talk to me. She knows who I am and that I live a long way off but does not know where I live or how I get back and forth. She knows that I come to see her on occasion but cannot remember when the last time was or the time before that. She cannot remember what was just said and yet she can carry on a conversation. Whatever its subject—the conversation gets repeated over and over and over. She loves me and trusts me and is totally vulnerable.

I have come, partly, to sign fiduciary papers, take tighter financial control, and to do what is necessary to manage her estate. She does not know what I know, and I cannot tell her: There are dangers all around her and closer than she could imagine.

In Tookoolito's time, on Baffin Island, my mother would long since have been put into a death igloo and sealed up with a bit of caribou meat and a bit of seal blubber. Her family would have left for the next hunting ground. But now we in her family do what we can to maintain her in the loneliness that kills her. We visit when we can, never enough. We run her home by re-mote control. During the week, a nurse comes every day, from eight until eight. My mother is alone, by her request, at night. On weekends, one of us stays with her or has her with us; if that is not possible, the nurse comes.

I set my suitcase down. I take out recent photographs of spring flowers at home. See the azaleas, I say, the rhododendrons, the tulips, the fuchsia. She does not understand where they are. She says she wants to pay my car fare. I need an interpreter. I need help. Her floe is getting smaller, shrinking as it rushes toward the open ocean to the south. Water is lapping at our feet. "It's headed south," commentators say of the stock market. But my mother's floe, with its chintzes and flowers and the Marie Laurencin portrait of the forever little girl in the sun hat, is truly headed south. She has gotten to the bottom of Davis Strait. Soon she will meet the Atlantic Ocean. My brother, who fol-lows astrology, says it will be soon, as soon as next month. There is no rescue, no return. From the North Pole, there is only one direction.

I return to Bellingham, my new home in Washington.

Jumping back over to Tookoolito's floe, I find it is February 3, 1873. There is thick snow and light wind from the west. The temperature is fifteen degrees below zero. This warming trend might indicate that the floe has moved toward the Greenland coast, always warmer than the stormier Baffin

Island side. There is nothing to see but ice and icebergs in all their manifold and fantastic shapes.

According to Scoresby, the most abundant source of icebergs in arctic regions is the glaciers that feed into Baffin Bay. Some of these bergs were so large that, when they grounded, they lasted for some years and were named by the whalers. Chief nursery of troublesome bergs was Melville Bay, the indentation on the northwest coast of Greenland first known by the whalers as "Bergy Hole."

Close company to the *Polaris* party, icebergs were a constant but changing scenery, a diversion and an inspiration. For the Inuit, they were the home of the keepers of polar bear souls. For Tyson, they were metaphors for human life:

> *The berg (after breaking off from its parent glacier) then sails off, and, like the human race, each one fulfills its own destiny. Some are grounded, perhaps, not many miles from their birthplace; others travel on, and get shored up on a floe like this, and keep it company, as ours have done, for hundreds of leagues; others pursue their solitary and majestic course toward the open sea, and gently melt away their lives in the deep swell of the Atlantic. . . .*

The temperature dropped again, the snow increased, and all thoughts were on one subject: seals, the essential but elusive food that swam just below them—the hot blood and the burnable blubber, the sweet meat at play in their locked basement. Once more the Inuit families, nearing starvation, feared the "men." And once more, Tyson's thoughts darkened. On February 4, in his field book, he again lambasted Budington for his treachery, "leaving nineteen Souls on the Pack Ice to perish."

The next day, Ebierbing and Hans brought home a seal. Its capture was unusual and daring. The seal had stuck its head through young ice to gaze at the sun. Dazed, or charmed, it was lacking normal caution. Ebierbing shot it. Hans then got into the kyack, which he propelled by paddle and movements of his body over the young, fragile ice the sixty yards to the body of the seal. He secured it and dragged it back behind the kyack through ice that never would have borne the weight of a hunter, even a thin and hungry one.

The small seal, as precious as a finger of Sedna's, saved them. Every bit but bone and gall was eaten—every hair, and the greasy water in which it was cooked. Some of the blood was saved by pouring it into hollows in the ice.

"Anything is good that don't poison you," Ebierbing remarked.

And then, two days later, the miracle, again: Hans brought home a seal. Each hunter also shot a narwhal, but both animals sank.

Narwhals, called sea unicorns, were moving north as cracks in the ice widened. The whalers had a saying: "After seals unies, after unicorns whales." The spring migration north was beginning; the great wheel of life was moving.

The narwhal *(Monodon monoceros)* is a small gray-white whale measuring up to seventeen feet. The male has an unusual appendage—a spiral ivory tusk as long as nine or ten feet.

According to Inuit legend, the narwhal came into being when a young man killed his mother, who had abused him, by throwing her into the water as he harpooned a whale.

Monarchs prized narwhal tusks as symbols of protection and power. It was said that the King of Denmark had a throne made from the ivory of narwhals, while other rulers had scepters fashioned from their tusks. When Martin Frobisher returned from his voyage to Meta Incognita in 1577, he presented Queen Elizabeth with a narwhal tusk six feet long, for which she paid him 100 pounds. (He also presented her an Inuit man, woman, and child who soon died.) The curious tooth was long sought-after as an aphrodisiac and medicine. Greenlanders prized the flesh of the spotted whale.

Now, on the floe, there was trouble with Hans's seal. Hans wanted it for himself and his family. Tyson exploded, privately, in his notebook. Hans, he wrote, is "a very Selfish Thoughtless good for nothing Esquimaux he is no hunter and lacks but little of being a fool he Does not Know how to build a Hut to Shelter himself and family." He went on to accuse him of being a danger to be around. Hans had threatened not to hunt anymore. Let him, Tyson countercharged: He would allow him nothing to eat, and Hans would go hungry.

As with so many other matters, it depends on which source you read, which lens you look through. Tip the magnifying glass slightly and the terrain of words shifts as if by tectonic upheaval. Introduce refraction, and the image metamorphoses. Add time, and the record wears away, ridge after ridge crumbling until finally there is nothing left but stardust.

Hans was not really Hans Hendrick but Suersaq, an Inuk born near Fiskernaes in southern Greenland in 1834. He married into the Polar Inuit of Smith Sound—the farthest north tribe—and spent many years among them. He had accompanied both Kane and Hayes on their expeditions before joining the *Polaris* on its way north up the Greenland coast. He had abandoned Kane's party, in desperate circumstances, in order to marry Mersek, the mother of his four children. Six years later, on the Hayes expedition of 1860–61, he had been traveling with fellow expedition member and astronomer August Sonntag, when Sonntag fell into the water and froze to death. Hans was blamed for the death, his reputation forever darkened. In his journal outburst, Tyson said it was no wonder that Sonntag had frozen to death while with Hans.

Within their contexts, the problems with the two earlier expeditions are explainable, understandable, and, with a certain angle of vision—a certain tipping of the magnifying glass—can be passed over without blame. But there was always the explaining that had to be done, always the shadow that hung; and to boot Hans's ability as a hunter was nowhere near that of Ebierbing's.

The truth is that Hans was a concern and an irritant to Tyson. What his relationship was with Ebierbing and Tookoolito we cannot know. Surely the men bonded as they hunted. In spite of all their differences, they must have felt a kinship. But no magnifying glass can be put to their hearts any more than to ours. There is no researcher's tool such as the 5x LumiLoupe that "allows ambient light to illuminate the subject for bright, clear viewing. Perfect for insects, plants, maps, and books!"

At night, the noise-making narwhals blew in the holes and cracks of the ice, and by day the men continued to hunt them. Hans went back to work, but a whaling harpoon formerly on the floe had long since been broken up for firewood, and a narwhal could not be obtained without one. Just enough seals came aboard the floe to keep the castaways alive. Tyson brought in stores of both fresh and saltwater ice, which could be gotten from various places on the floe. The salt ice was melted to season the "soup" or "tea," while the fresh provided drinking water.

Hall's rifle had gone to Hans. Tyson had asked him to keep it safe until he could use it. Now, on asking for it, he learned it had gone to one of the men and was broken. The unnamed man refused to give it up. Tyson complained:

They (the men) took possession of everything from the first, and are very insolent and do as they please; and as I am entirely alone, I see no way to enforce obedience without shedding blood; and should I do that and live, it is easy to see my life would be sworn away should we ever get home. These wretched men will bring ruin on themselves and the whole party yet, I fear.

The wind blew from the south and the north; the wind died down. All the while, the currents were pulling hard to the south. Snow accompanied the gales, sometimes burying the prisoners in their huts. When the skies cleared, the sun was now high enough that it shone through the ice window in the igloo that Tyson shared with Tookoolito and Ebierbing. Though it was welcome, the new light came at a price, revealing the execrable state of their home and condition. It caused Punny one morning to stare at Tyson and remark, "You are nothing but bone!" The light also stirred the men to carry out of their hut the equivalent of a cartload of black, smoky ice.

Icicles of condensation were knocked from the walls, and the "carpet" of canvas in Tookoolito and Ebierbing's snow house was taken outside and shaken and beaten. Nothing could remove the grime of blood, blubber, grease, and saliva. Nothing could clean clothes, equipment, or bodies. The cooking pan was cleaned with fingers or tongue, the traditional method. Ebierbing remarked that white men consider the Inuit filthy but that the men in the adjoining igloo were far worse. It can be assumed that their passageway, used as a latrine, was also in need of a thorough cleaning.

For personal hygiene, Tyson borrowed a rough comb of Tookoolito's every morning to get his hair under control; there was nothing more that could be done. He began to long for clean underclothes more than anything. Getting clean had entered the realm of fantasy and obsession; Tyson was giving increasing expression to it.

February 15 marked the four-month anniversary of their separation from the *Polaris*. There were minimal provisions for one more month. Foxes had returned—another sign of spring. But seal meat was lacking. Tyson started cutting back on his rations of bread and pemmican and gave to Punny part of what was his.

February 16, Herron noted:

Wind W.S.W.; 16° below zero. Saw plenty of whales; wish they would take their departure; they frighten the seals away, which we are now so badly in want of; our provisions are getting very low. When you take a glass and look around, you see the ice in the distance piled up as high as a ship's mast, so that it seems impossible to travel over it—certainly not with a boat—and no land to be seen yet. We want water to escape, and, please God, we will get it when the time comes.

That same day, having finally obtained a rifle, Tyson started out hunting, though his threadbare and inadequate clothes would not keep out the wind. When he returned for lunch, Tookoolito had his meal ready—a piece of seal flipper and a pot of seal-blood soup. It was, he said, "quite a heavy lunch."

Now there were at least three men out hunting on a daily basis. The results came slowly. February 17, Hans got a seal, a small one. Ebierbing got a dovekie, while one of the "Germans" bagged two. Each of the little speckled birds with their plaintive cry would provide about four ounces of meat; it would take sixty-six of them to provide two meals a day for the group. During his earlier expedition, Hayes claimed that he "would not for the world have hurt a feather of their trembling little heads," but he was not starving on a floe.

On February 19, the west coast—Baffin Island—came into sight. It was what Tyson had longed for, but there was no way to get there. As compensation, Ebierbing secured a seal, which Tyson looked forward to apportioning equally, along with a tenth of a pound of bread to each. But the men grabbed the small animal and divided it up as they chose. Ebierbing remarked that he ought to be paid $100 for each seal taken from him, and Tyson heartily agreed. The land of commerce and fair exchange, however, began more than forty miles away; it might as well have been in the next galaxy.

The following day, the three hunters secured eleven dovekies. Two bags of bread and three cans of pemmican remained. The day after, there was no success in hunting. Seals and narwhals could be seen but not caught. Lunch consisted of a dovekie and a piece of blubber. Tyson was having the boat repaired; at any time the weather might enable—or require—them to move off the floe and attempt to reach land. The men were frightened. They were so weak it took several of them to carry the kyack, and a number of them who had tried to move the boat had failed to budge it.

Ebierbing was frightened, too. How could he possibly provide for his family when he had all these others as well, men who would stop at nothing to fill their stomachs? The west coast, as he and Tyson both knew, was desolate and formidable. What would they do if they managed to get there? To reach land and escape from the men still seemed the only course. At least, that way, he would have the hope of saving his family from a fate worse than starvation.

On February 23, Tyson told the men that as soon as the weather permitted, they would start for the shore. They would aim for a place that the Inuit called Shaumeer, just to the north of Cape Mercy, at 65° north. Game was known to be there, and possibly people. Cape Mercy marked the northern entrance to Cumberland Sound.

Preparations were begun. The tent was enlarged. Ammunition was divided into several bags and put in different places, for protection. Tyson was determined that the party would be as well prepared as possible for the eventual shift to the boat.

Soon, he told the men, they would reach the bearded seal, or *oogjook.* This large seal *(Erignathus barbatus)* with heavy jaw and thick whiskers spends the winter on the pack and gives birth on the ice from mid-March to late April. The males are known for a unique underwater song. Females as well as males reach a weight of up to 750 pounds. Capturing one would mean a feast for the starving drifters and temporary relief. In the meantime, daily rations were reduced even further, down to one meal a day, and consisted now of five-and-a-half pounds of bread and four pounds of pemmican for the whole group.

Then, March 2, deliverance! Ebierbing shot and secured the long-awaited bearded seal. Tyson said it was the largest he had ever seen—approximately 600 to 700 pounds, capable of producing 30 gallons of oil. When measured, it proved nine feet long, including the hind flipper. If they had been under more normal circumstances, the Inuit would have stretched, dried, and cut the skin into strips for sledge tracings and lashings and the lines used to secure walrus. This was the strongest natural material in the northern world. But now, on the floe, there was thought of only one activity: eating. Johnson, representing every member of the colony, danced and sang for joy. (It was Johnson who sometimes at night, if there had been food, spun a sailor's yarn after the men had lain down.) Tookoolito had only two small pieces of blubber left for the lamp, enough for two days. Mersek had enough for one. The men had even less. If not for the seal, they would have soon been in darkness and without any means of warmth.

An orgy began. In all three huts, butchering, cooking, and eating took over. All hands and faces were smeared with blood. The men could not be restrained, and some of them ate until they were sick. Only the day before, they had been subsisting on nine ounces a day. Now there was more than they could eat.

Still, there was no mistaking the perilous nature of the floating slaughterhouse. It must have been painful indeed when the floe approached Cumberland Sound, Tookoolito and Ebierbing's home, and the place where Tyson first had met them so many years before. This place of youth, whales, conjunction, dreams, and promise, the place that had bloomed into trips abroad, was there, just over the ice, a refuge of islands and anchorages.

Have you passed by your childhood home when it was shut off from you forever? I have. Mine was on Long Island: a Revolutionary period white clapboard with shutters and wisteria, surrounded by locust and horse chestnut trees, with a haunted cemetery at the top of the apple orchard. When my father, in the process of divorcing my mother, sold it illegally, taking the proceeds from my mother, she was cast aside. She went to live with her older sister Virginia, who willed her her apartment and estate.

I have passed by the house and have been close to capsized by emotion. Much earlier, when I drove away from that house after my wedding reception, I could never have foretold where the currents would carry me—to Alaska and a new interior landscape. That inside terrain was as different to me as the wild mountains of Juneau, which became my home for twenty-seven years.

As she approached Cape Mercy, Tookoolito had to be remembering her family, her marriage to Ebierbing, her trip to England, and the winter Margaret Penny visited Cumberland Sound, bringing back to life all the memories of the season in London, bringing back the ceremony of tea. How Tookoolito must have longed for tea now, replaying those scenes of gentler life over and over, those days of cleanliness and kindness.

This, I know, was the time of Tookoolito's greatest heroism. This was the deciding battle. Everything in her, all of her training and instinct, must have told her to bolt—to run from the "Germans," to run from Tyson, who was such a different companion from Father Hall, to run to what she knew in the ice-locked coves of Cumberland Sound. But she didn't. A long time ago, she had signed on to serve the expedition. The expedition was not over; Father Hall's work was not finished. It was not yet time to go home. Here, Too-koolito took the secret helm, putting her back to what was familiar. She did more. She became for the floe what her people would have called a *tornaq*, an invisible ruler or guiding spirit. Her intent was now the driving force.

On the moving surface of the frozen sea, nothing appeared to have changed. The wind blew and snow drifted. Icebergs appeared and disappeared. For those burrowed into the vast and southbound whiteness, existence was still marked with desire and very occasional satisfaction. Ebierbing, remarkably, still had some tobacco. He gave two pipefuls to Tyson, now out, his last and only pleasure gone. On other hapless expeditions, coffee grounds, tea leaves, even rope and cotton have been substituted for tobacco, but none of these was available.

The land disappeared from sight, and the weather grew much colder again. On March 5, Ebierbing split up pieces of meat by whacking them with a hammer; they had been sitting within one foot of the lamp fire for thirty hours. Tyson found the frozen meat much too hard to eat. Dinner that evening consisted of part of the oogjook's head and a pot of blood. For the first time, in his journal, Tyson admitted thoughts of suicide, cut short by a recital of Christian doctrine. If he had discussed the subject with Tookoolito, he would have learned that her people believed suicides went to heaven; maybe then he would have been less certain.

By the next day, the wind was more severe than any they had experienced so far. The party was buried in snow and had to dig and cut their way out—then were quickly driven back inside with frozen faces. Only the providential oogjook kept them from death.

The winds and currents were carrying them toward more oogjooks but also toward breakup and open water. It might be that they could overcome the challenge of starvation only to succumb to exposure and drowning. A southerly gale could explode their ice prison at any moment. Already, their floor was cracking and snapping beneath them. The phenomenon was not an earthquake but a seaquake. Loose chunks of ice were crashing up against their feet.

March 8, Tyson roamed ten miles over the floe looking for open water but found only solid ice. By evening, Hans had not returned from hunting. "This Hans is a plague," Tyson remarked.

Tyson was not feeling well; the all-meat diet did not agree with him. And the men had all been sick for a week. Tyson had told them not to eat the liver of the oogjook—it was poisonous, as the liver of the polar bear was—but they insisted on eating it anyway. Now they were all afflicted, first with headaches, then with the skin peeling off their faces, chests, and hands.

The winds increased and the seaquake strengthened. The epicenter seemed to be immediately beneath them. The night of March 10, at about 9:00, a nearby crash drew Tyson and Ebierbing out of their hut. Feeling their way in the darkness, they found that the ice had broken twenty yards away, the two edges grinding and slamming against each other. The gale continued for sixty hours—a long, violent unbirthing of the floe.

March 12, the weather moderated, and the prisoners could see: What had been relatively smooth floes had become a pack—huge blocks of ice all piled and jumbled together in unimaginable confusion. But there was open water. By the end of the day, there were also four seals to eat.

A respite. The floe drifted along peacefully. Meyer said their position was 64°32' north; if true, they would have been directly east of Cumberland Sound. For the time being, the ice island, though smaller, was stable. All its passengers were well. Little Tobias had recovered. The icebergs that accompanied them might have been the subject of an artist's delight, but their beauty and majesty were lost on their audience. By March 14, Ebierbing and Tyson could stand in the door of their hut to shoot seals. Soon after sunrise, Tyson caught sight of an oogjook. While beckoning Ebierbing, the better shot, to come along with his Springfield rifle, he whistled to catch the animal's attention. The oogjook, entranced, waited until Ebierbing could take his fatal shot.

It was now, on March 15, five months since the Separation. Despite their attempts at "spring cleaning," the camp had become insufferably dirty. Tyson was eager to place blame and found an easy target in Tookoolito. In his field book, he released his venom:

> . . . *I cannot describe to you how dirty and nasty it is. I know it is impossible to be very clean living as we do, but I must tell the thruth [sic]. This Esquimaux squaw Hannah is the dirtiest, most filthy thing I have ever*

seen. She is filthy for an Esquimaux. I have never seen her equall as a dirty & lazy squaw. And this squaw has been home living with civilized people.

In the edited, published version, Tyson softened the description and added an explanation:

But among the Americans Hannah learned one thing that has been of no benefit to her, and which has added many annoyances to our inevitable discomfort the past winter. She observed among the white folks that it was the custom for men to support their wives, instead of using them as slaves, as her own people do in their natural condition; and, in order to be as much like a white woman as possible, she has positively declined to do— has certainly omitted to do—many things which would have made this hut more tolerable.

I think of a different view, the magnifying glass tipped to another angle. In late October 1865, as Hall prepared to set out with Tookoolito and Ebierbing for King William's Land in the spring, a terrible gale blew for five days. Tookoolito remembered a woman she had met at the Brooklyn Fair who wanted Inuit people to dress like her and remarked: "I'd like to see her take a minute's walk over the hill. She'd be glad to exchange her fine hat and hoop skirts for any of our rough dresses."

Tookoolito, igloo-wife, knew what to do. There was a place for dresses and there was a place for suits made of caribou skin. It was like jumping from floe to floe; you adjusted to the circumstances and reestablished your balance. Tookoolito had been doing it all of her life. Her life, indeed, depended on knowing just when and where to jump. Tookoolito's roof was made of sky, her floor of frozen sea. Her walls were made of snow. When she looked out, it was through a window made of ice—a lens into the history and the alchemy of stars.

Chapter Nine

March 16, 1873–March 29, 1873

POLAR BEARS: THE POWER BEYOND LIFE

After returning home, to the other side of the country, I called my mother. She was concerned that her feet were swollen. She asked if I knew what to do. And then asked again. No, I felt like saying. I am not captain of this ship. I do not have to be responsible for feet—swollen, frostbitten, gangrenous, nails peeling off with the cold. I do not have to amputate.

Sometimes in the Arctic, European sailors would return from a trek across ice with their feet frozen rock solid. As they regained the deck, they would stomp as if with wooden blocks. They would have to be restrained from going right to the fire; only slow thawing could possibly save them. As their limbs warmed, their feet would become so swollen they would have to be cut out of their boots. A frozen foot would swell to the size of a football. The pain would be intense. Then the flesh would begin to rot away. The agonizingly slow, predictable march of gangrene up the leg could rarely be halted, even by amputation. The ice journals are filled with examples of these protracted deaths and the amputations intended to forestall them.

British "discovery" ships had surgeons on board. After the middle of the nineteenth century, British whalers were also required to have surgeons on board. These "surgeons," usually medical students looking for adventure and expenses for their schooling, tended to be young and inexperienced but bright and observant. One was Arthur Conan Doyle, who sailed at the age of twenty to the coast of Greenland aboard the whaler *Hope* in 1880.

If there were no surgeons aboard, amputation fell to the lot of the captain. And sometimes, self-amputation was the only answer. Peter Freuchen had returned to camp on Danish Island at the east entrance to Repulse Bay after being trapped in a snow cave, his left foot frozen. He received treatment from an Inuit woman who claimed to have a great deal of experience taking care of frostbite victims. Her treatment included placing the still-warm skins of lemmings, bloody side down, on his foot. Every time she changed the dressing, some of the rotting skin peeled off. The gangrene did not spread beyond his toes; however, it left him with bare bones. Because he could not stand the sight of them, he fitted a pair of pincers around each toe, hitting them with a hammer to remove them one by one.

Local lore also helped an American explorer. Dr. Isaac I. Hayes, traveling with Kane in the second United States Grinnell expedition of 1853–55, returned from an impromptu fox chase with his stockinged feet frozen. Their color was that "of a tallow candle." Because the frost had not penetrated deeply, however, he was able to put to good use the Inuit method he had learned: application of ice-cold water followed by rubbing with the feathery side of a bird skin. He escaped, as he says, with a few blisters. But only to be caught again.

Damage done by the cold goes deep and lasts long. Hall, luckily, never succumbed to frostbite, largely because of the tutelage of Tookoolito, with whom he started traveling his first northern winter. During their first morning out, she watched his face carefully. When telltale signs appeared, she applied her warm hands to the dangerous patches. She taught him the trick of solo travel: Keep looking at your face in a mirror. He borrowed hers, and he says, "I found the use of a mirror in such a case equivalent to the companionship of another person."

A mirror can save a face from frostbite but is no equivalent to companionship. Lack of companionship can kill just as cold can kill.

My mother, her life circumscribed and protected, was dying of loneliness when she first collapsed more than a year ago. Her last good friend, Edith, had died. She had no one with whom to go out. Movies, exercise classes, walks fell away. The circumference of her space got smaller and smaller. Now it is worn away to her small co-op in a building contiguous with the Russian Consulate and across the street from the Spence School. She has a doorman named Angel. There is one named Lloyd, from Belize. There are also Danny, Alex, and Amano. The Superintendent is Mike, from Ireland.

From the front door, these guardians can look out on the streams of people that flow by on Madison and Fifth Avenues. If those people were seals, the doormen could harpoon them and haul them in. They could be butchered there in the foyer, under the fresh flowers, and distributed throughout the building, evenly and fairly, the same share to each. The hunters then could light a blubber lamp under the marquee for a beacon. My mother is that close to the edge.

The East River—up which the *Polaris* steamed on her way from the Brooklyn Navy Yard to the North Pole—is only a pleasant walk away. Its huge current pulls to the Atlantic Ocean; that, too, is but a short distance. Stepping outside of my mother's building, I could easily reach the Atlantic by subway, taxi, or bus. I cannot tell what the weather is there. From the middle of the ice floe, it is almost impossible to know what lies beyond its edge. A gale could be blowing while it is calm in the center of the ice. Sailors used to say of this phenomenon, "the frost kills the wind."

But I do not go to the ocean. When I visit, I stay in my mother's neighborhood—the center of the floe—doing small errands, keeping close. Not very long ago, I would walk with her, but now she hardly walks at all. Throughout her neighborhood, I see old women being walked and pushed in wheelchairs by assistants, who are usually of another race. Nearly always, the old woman is Caucasian, her companion Hispanic or African-American. The old woman is wealthy and cared for but alone and dependent.

I wonder if I have abandoned my mother. Once, in early spring in the

Conservatory Garden in New York, I sat with her on a bench inscribed, "In loving memory of Priscilla G., 1970–91, from A.G.M. who adored her." The magnolia tree in front of us, festooned with sparrows, had just begun to bloom. I have sat with my mother on many memorial benches but have always remembered that particular one, that day. We had just come from an exhibit of ancient Greek sculpture at the Metropolitan Museum of Art. Friends, who showed us the exhibit, took us to lunch at the members' restaurant. It was then I became aware of my mother's loss of memory; there were certain questions she could not answer. In the funeral steles we had looked at, stone figures wave goodbye without looking into one another's eyes. Had I looked into my mother's eyes that day, or away? Could I bring myself to say goodbye while there was still time? If, like the Inuit, I could not say goodbye, could I at least say *Terbouetie?*

After my mother's friend Edith died, my mother often talked of getting a park bench inscribed in her memory. I never did anything about it, and now my mother no longer mentions Edith.

Back on the *Polaris* floe, it was March 17, 1873—five months into the drift. Recent days had passed with clouds, wind, snow, and the consistently uncatchable narwhals, which might have been as mythical as the unicorns for which they were named. Now, suddenly, there was a vigorous but unsuccessful chase after a bear. Bears had been coming closer to the huts at night, sometimes within twenty paces, but this was the first one observed in daylight.

According to noontime observations, the latitude was 63°47' north—a drift of thirty-two miles in the last three days. The unwilling passengers were now opposite the islands off the mouth of Frobisher Bay: the Dreaded Land.

March 21—the Equinox—brought continuing cold winds from the northwest. But it was a banner day. Ebierbing managed to secure six seals and Hans one. The ice village, again, was turned to a scene of carnage. Still, according to Tyson, the men were not satisfied:

> *These Germans are tremendous eaters and outrageous grumblers. They seem to be possessed with the idea that they can improve everything—as they did the useful harpoon into a useless spear, and, in consequence, nearly every rifle we had upon the ice but Joe's, which they could not get hold of, has been ruined by their tinkering. They must work away at everything, and never stop till it is rendered useless.*

With the sun in Aries, the weather was still wintery, and the water around them had frozen solid once more, to a distance of a mile or more, cutting them off from seals. But there were bear tracks everywhere. The temperature was zero, and, when Tyson tried to hunt, he had to give up because of rheumatism. He was encouraged, however, by the southward drift. At 61°59' north, he maintained, they were nearing the realm of the "bladder-nose" seal.

The hooded or crested seal *(Cystophora cristata)* is known as the "bladder-nose" because of the extraordinary membranous balloon that the males can distend through the left nostril. When excited, the male can also inflate his "hood," an enlargement of the nasal cavity, which swells to form a large sac over his head. The males weigh up to 900 pounds, the females over 600 pounds. The pups are born, on the ice, from mid-March to early April, and nurse for only three to five days. As soon as the pup is weaned, the female goes immediately into oestrus. She is, as a result, always attended during the time of birthing and nursing by one or more bulls, none of which is likely to be the sire of the pup. These family groups, Tyson knew, would be showing up soon.

On March 26, he was proved right. Between them, Ebierbing and Hans shot nine and secured four of the monsters—enough meat for eighteen or twenty days. A whale was also seen: further proof that they had entered the rich waters where both food and rescue were possible.

The floe party was now, indeed, entering the strong tides of the mouth of Hudson Strait, between the south end of Baffin Island and the north tip of the coast of Labrador (now called Newfoundland). This is where, in 1578, Frobisher sailed off course into an unknown body of water. Calling it his "Mistaken Strait," he backed out and left possession to the mariner who would follow thirty-two years later, Henry Hudson. This is also where Frobisher's fleet of tiny ships was caught up in a voracious riptide. Icebergs, whirlpools, storms, and fog assailed them like the furies of hell. Here, his mariners fell down on icy decks to pray for deliverance.

On March 28, Tyson's "fools of fortune," as he called his charges, got their bear—but only, as might be expected, after a perilous encounter. It was shortly after dark, and the inhabitants of Tookoolito's igloo were preparing for bed. Tyson had just taken off his boots. Suddenly there was a noise like the breaking of ice. Ebierbing went out to assess the situation but quickly returned, clearly frightened, with the news that there was a bear by his kyack, ten feet away from the igloo. The rifles were outside, where they were always kept to protect them from the condensation inside. Only Ebierbing's pistol was within. Tyson put his boots back on and went outside with Ebierbing. At the entrance, they could hear the bear eating the seal skins and blubber lying unprotected near the kyack. Ebierbing crept into the men's hut to warn them. Tyson got to his rifle but, in grabbing it, knocked down a shotgun beside it. The bear growled and started for him. Tyson pulled the trigger. Nothing happened. And again. And again. Running for his life, he got into the igloo, reloaded the rifle, crept out again, and took a shot in the dark. It reached its mark just as Ebierbing came out of the men's hut and shot at the bear with both his pistol and rifle. The bear continued to run, then fell dead. In the morning, while skinning him, Tyson found that his shot-in-the-dark bullet had entered the animal's left shoulder and passed through the heart. Except for the poisonous liver, overloaded with vitamin A, every part of the healthy young bear was eaten—a grateful change in diet.

Ursus maritimus, the polar bear, ceaselessly wanders the moving ice. Only the female periodically settles down, every third year, to give birth in a chambered den much like an Inuit igloo. Perhaps it is because a cub is born tiny, blind, and toothless—as helpless as a kitten; perhaps it is because the mother has fasted in isolation in the den for approximately six months during gestation, birth, and early nursing; perhaps it is because the cub, or cubs (usually twins), stay with their mother for up to two-and-a-half years, forming a strong bond; or, perhaps there is something else, lying beyond empirical evidence, the something else that gives rise to myth and totemic allegiance. Whatever it is, the attachment is extraordinary.

Almost every chronicler of the Arctic, from earliest times, has a story of the ferocious affection between a mother bear and her cubs. Samuel Taylor Coleridge, who read and made use of the first histories of arctic travel, grasped the image of this fierce bond at an early stage in his writing:

> *And first a landscape rose*
> *More wild and waste and desolate than where*
> *The white bear, drifting on a field of ice,*

Howls to her sundered cubs with piteous rage
And savage agony.
"THE DESTINY OF NATIONS"

A mother polar bear, however, is not likely to be separated for long from her cubs and will ruthlessly protect them from danger. Scoresby and other chroniclers provide numerous accounts of what lengths a sow will go to to guard her young, often losing her life in the process. When threatened, she will push her cubs in front of her, carrying, pushing, or pitching them forward as necessary. When the dogs are upon them, she will sit on her haunches and, with the cubs between her hind legs, fight off the dogs with her front paws while roaring. The mother or cub, whichever survives the first bullets, will ferociously protect the body of the fallen. Cubs are reported trying to suckle as their mother is being skinned and dying sows directing their last look at their still-living cubs.

In May 1862, while Hall was exploring Frobisher Bay, he learned just how fierce a mother bear could be. He and his party had encountered a sow and her cub. In the chase, the two became separated. The eleven dogs went after the cub. When the cub made a rush at Hall, he speared it and then clubbed it to death. His companions, who had set out after the mother and failed to stop her, were not pleased when they returned and discovered what he had done. They feared that the mother bear would return and attack the party in the night.

What comes through in so many of these tales is the theme not just of fierceness but of affection. Commentators sometimes cannot help lapsing into human terms. Captain Gravill of the *Diana* tells of a captured cub that would not settle down until its mother's body had been hoisted on board:

It laid down beside her and moaned and sobbed most pitiful, and licked the blood from her wounds and tried to lift her head up with its paws. 'Twas most distressing to look at.

Such young bears could be sold to zoological gardens for up to £20.

To kill a polar bear was a significant accomplishment that also required significant tribute. As Hall learned during his first expedition, the ritual must be carefully followed. If the captured bear was male, his bladder had to be placed on the top of an igloo or tupic for three days and three nights along with certain instruments of the men. If female, the bladder had to be hung with one of the women's brass head ornaments and some beads. If the bear ws captured during a sea trip, the bladder had to be hung from the mast or a pole in the boat as the party traveled. Hall sailed with such a talisman in August 1861 as he explored Frobisher Bay, the stomachs of all in the party filled with the treat of sweet bear meat.

Powerful in death as in life, the polar bear was considered a vital guardian: A young child was thought to be protected by the tooth of a bear sewed to the back of its shirt. The tooth must not be lost, because it keeps the soul from danger.

The bond between polar bear and cub figures in age-old stories. One of them is told by Hall, who said it was a tradition credited by the Inuit from above Cumberland Sound to Hudson's Strait, and from Igloolik to Chester-field Inlet. As the story goes, an Inuit woman was said to have obtained a po-lar bear cub newly born and raised it as a pet. When the cub grew to be the best hunter in the area, the woman's neighbors became jealous and threat-ened to kill him. The woman, to save his life, asked him to leave but to con-tinue hunting for her, and he did, for the rest of her life.

Back on the *Polaris* floe, after the polar bear was shot on March 28, there was much feasting. Its fat, Herron noted, "cuts like gelatine." The men par-ticularly enjoyed making sausages from the tender and tasteful meat. Then, the wind sprang up fiercely from the northwest, and the respite was over. Soon the wind had become a gale, tearing at the ice. During the twenty-ninth, huge bergs surrounded and threatened the chunk to which the pris-oners clung. "We are completely hemmed in by them," Herron said. One enormous berg actually collided with the ice raft but did no fatal damage. Improbably, the fragile vessel sailed on, into increasingly heavy seas and even greater challenge.

Five and one-half months the captive mariners had survived—only to meet their greatest danger: rising water.

Chapter Ten

March 30, 1873–June 5, 1873

END THINGS

Ebierbing, Punny, Tookoolito

What does it look like at the edge of the ice, or at the rim of the hole in the sky? Ice kills the wind; you cannot tell what lies beyond. Refraction transmogrifies the terrain; you cannot tell whether you are looking at a bear, a bird, or a hill. Near the Magnetic Pole, the compass swings; and, at the North Pole, what time could it possibly be?

In the city, it is important to remember to look up—past the confusions of people and the limitations of buildings. There are holes in the sky, where the birds go, where sometimes you want to follow. Sometimes you want to say, "North, north, I am inclined to walk the sky to its hole, the birds to their country. What is there, in that hole, where midnight nests?"

By March 30, 1873, the *Polaris* floe was reduced to a sliver. Its crew would soon have to abandon it, becoming marine gypsies as well as castaways. In the meantime, two "bladder-noses" were secured, a female and her pup. Later, Hans shot another young one. The milk in the stomach of the young was highly prized. The men added some to their blood soup.

April 1: In Cumberland Sound, the date would have been known as the Moon for the Birth of the Young Seal. On the floe, however, thoughts of hunting, cooking, and eating had to be put aside. The wanderers were now at 59°41' north, in the lower part of the Labrador Sea, at the threshold of the Atlantic Ocean. It is as hard to tell where one body of water ends and the next begins as it is to tell in a snowstorm where one flake ends and the next begins. Who can say where we are? Physicists now argue how many dimensions—eleven, some say—govern the universe; still, no matter what the magnitude, everything comes from one perfect substance and lives in motion.

The name of the water hardly mattered. The "fools of fortune" would soon be swamped. Their tiny piece of ice was now entirely detached from the main pack, which lay to the west. Their situation was so perilous that they needed to take action—a dangerous and dramatic step. They would attempt to regain the pack, Tyson decided, in spite of the risk. To do this, they would have to get in the boat carrying as little as possible. Much of their supply of meat would have to be left behind. They would also have to jettison much of the ammunition, because of its weight. They could carry only their tent and the animal skins essential for protection against the weather. Tyson insisted on taking Hall's writing desk, all that was left of their commander. Some of the men tried to get Ebierbing, who had protected it all this time, to throw it overboard.

Tyson gave little previous warning or opportunity for discussion. He knew the group had to abandon their floating home or be drowned; this was no time for debate. He also knew where they had to go. Some wanted to head away from the pack, by heading south, into open water, but he knew the relative security of solid ice was essential—for protection from the open ocean, for food, and for drinking water.

Crammed into a boat designed for six or eight, at the most, the party of nineteen managed to make approximately twenty miles west toward the pack. While underway, they took so much water over the sides that some of the men panicked and cried out that the boat was sinking. Tyson ordered all of the seal meat thrown overboard. They had urgent need of it but even greater need to keep the party intact and afloat. He was afraid, from the expression in some of the men's eyes, that they were ready to throw the women and children overboard to save themselves.

Almost engulfed, children crying, Tyson at his wits' end, the refugees had to take hold of the first decent slab of ice they could find. Once on it, the group set up the tent, spread out what skins they had, and ate a small bit of dry bread and pemmican. Hans and his family were assigned the boat for sleeping.

The next day, April 2, the party set out again in search of a more secure home. They did what they could to push west but were propelled back by wind and snow blowing from that quarter. The best they could make was south-southwest. Exhausted, they hauled up again on another chunk of ice and made camp.

On April 3, the castaways spent considerable time repairing the boat and rigging up canvas washboards to keep water from spilling in. Then they were on their way again, struggling toward the pack to the west. On April 4, they regained it and disembarked. While Ebierbing searched for snow out of which to cut blocks for an igloo, Meyer got out his instruments and determined that their new latitude was 56°47' north.

They were making progress. Their new platform was heavy. For the moment they were safe. But, of course, nothing was safe in spring at the edge of an ice pack at the edge of the open sea with water rising all around.

By April 5, a gale was blowing from the northeast, and heavy swells tore at the ice. The floe began to break apart. Everything had to be hauled to the center. Then Ebierbing and Tookoolito's hut was washed away, with just enough warning that they were able to escape with Punny and some few things they had with them. There was no telling where, or when, the next crack would strike, or the next swell that might wash them all away. Ebierbing rebuilt his temporary home, but there was really nothing for anyone to do but wait and worry. A watch was set, but truly everyone old enough to recognize the situation was on watch, peering with deep fear into the ocean's dark jaws. There could be no rest.

The gale, now blowing from the northwest, strengthened the next day and kept the party imprisoned. Tookoolito and Ebierbing's second igloo was ripped away when the ice split right through the middle of it. Now, on the night of April 6, there was no room for the group to lie down. They stood by their boat, already loaded with their scant belongings, for a quick escape.

Wind and swell continued to build. At six in the morning of April 7, the ice split under the tent as a meager breakfast was being organized. The tent was saved but the meal was lost. The boat was almost lost.

In the commotion of these terrible days, there was no time nor opportunity to hunt. The transients were once more starving. Because there was no way to melt ice for water, they were also suffering acutely from thirst.

Half of the men got in under the tent to try to rest while the other half walked around it. Any sleep was quick and broken, the exhausted bodies tensed for flight, any sound a possible alarm.

Then, at midnight on the night of April 7–8, the ice split between the tent and the boat—so close together a person could not walk between them. Meyer was on the side with the boat and the kyack, Tyson on the side with the tent. They looked at each other through the blowing snow but said nothing. All around them the ice was breaking and crashing, slabs riding on top of slabs. Once more, it was the unmaking of their world, a planet blown apart. Tyson and Meyer stood at opposite poles, separated by angry ocean.

Not knowing how to save the boat or kyack, Meyer cast the kyack adrift, hoping it would reach the other side and that one of the hunters could secure it, get into it, and come back to assist him. But the kyack drifted away. Knowing well how critically important it was, Ebierbing and Hans went for it, leaping from one piece of broken ice to another. Farther and farther away they hopscotched across the chaotic field of ice, disappearing into the fading light. They failed to reach the kyack but did get to the boat.

By then it was dark. The cold had deepened, and with it, the ice. Split up for the first time since the night of the Separation, the party minus Meyer, Ebierbing, and Hans settled down to await the light. When it came, they saw their three comrades with the boat.

There was nothing to do but make the attempt to reunite the party. Tyson picked up a stick for balance and support and started over the uncertain ice, now a field of shifting cakes. Kruger, the man who had caused him so much grief, followed. Picking and jumping their perilous way, they reached their companions and the boat only to find that they, Hans, and

Ebierbing could not stir it. Meyer was too weak to be of any use. Tyson called over to the larger party. Two more men came. Still the boat could not be budged. Then all but two of the men came over. Finally, they could move the boat and succeeded in getting it back to the encampment. Meyer and Frederick Jamka fell in the water and were rescued. The kyack was found.

The party sorted itself out, moved their tent near the boat in the center of the ice, and had a small ration of pemmican and bread for breakfast. Ebierbing built another igloo alongside the tent. A watch was set and a quiet time for sleep followed. For some hours the weather cooperated. There was even enough sun to take an observation and set the latitude at 55°51' north—in the lower part of the Labrador Sea, halfway down the Newfoundland coast.

During the night of the ninth, the sea, running very high, washed the occupants out of their tents and their igloos. Everyone raced toward the boat in preparation for escape, but there could be no escape in such weather. The heavily laden boat could not have survived such tumultuous seas.

The women and children were ensconced in the boat. The others simply tried to keep upright. Water was pouring over the ice. There was no dry place.

Then, at 10:00 P.M., conditions quieted. The ice began to close around them again, expanding their domain and providing some stability; the open water had withdrawn. The wind and sea subsided. At midnight, the refugees once more put up their tent and sought sleep.

The next day, April 10, remained calm, enough so that the prisoners could take stock. Meyer was suffering from frostbite. His toes had frozen during his time alone by the boat; then he had fallen in the water. There was nothing that could be done for him under the circumstances.

Two more calm days followed. A fox, ravens, and other land birds gave hope of a coast nearby, but the prisoners could see nothing but ice. Two large bergs were close neighbors, looming over them. In rough conditions, they might have crashed down on the helpless group. Fortunately, all remained quiet. Except for the fact that everyone in the group was cold, starving, and dehydrated, their general condition had improved considerably. According to Meyer, they had drifted to 55°35' north.

April 13 was Easter Sunday. It was also an ice-locked day of hunger and cold, hopeless for travel and the capture of seals. Only a glorious display of the northern lights the previous night kept the party from a sense of total desolation.

Did Tyson mention Easter to Tookoolito? He does not say, and there is no way to know. He appears to be living in the tent with the men, now, and not in the igloo with Tookoolito and her family. I wonder if he wanted an excuse to separate from his Inuit family, or if, for tactical purposes, he thought it better to disassociate himself and also to monitor the dissidents? The men, of course, might have seized the boat, or attempted to, and made off without Tyson and the two families.

If Tookoolito thought of Easter, she might have kept it to herself. A day that was supposed to be a time of Resurrection was, for the drifters, a day of destitution. It is hard to hope for salvation when what you want to save is not your soul but your life—and your child's life. Undoubtedly, everyone on board had thoughts of what would come next. The Inuit had very definite ideas of what happens after death. As Tookoolito once explained it:

> *"My people think this way:* Koodleparmiung *(heaven) is upward. Everybody happy there. All the time light; no snow, no ice, no storms; always pleasant; no trouble; never tired; sing and play all the time—all this to continue without end.*
>
> *"Adleparmeun (hell) is downward. Always dark there. No sun; trouble there continually; snow flying all the time; terrible storms; cold, very cold; and a great deal of ice there. All who go there must always remain.*
>
> *"All Innuits who have been good go to Koodleparmiung; that is, who have been kind to the poor and hungry—all who have been happy while living on this earth. Any one who has been killed by accident, or who has committed suicide, certainly goes to the happy place.*
>
> *"All Innuits who have been bad—that is, unkind one to another—all who have been unhappy while on this earth, will go to Adleparmeun. If an Innuit kill another because he is mad at him, he will certainly go to Adleparmeun."*

Weakened by frostbite, Meyer was now close to death by starvation. With the provisions almost gone and hunting for seals impossible—the hunters could not move through or over the ice in its rotting condition—the situation was growing desperate. Tyson was moved to pity:

Poor Meyer looks wretchedly; the loss of food tells on him worse than on the rest. He looks very weak. I have much sympathy for him, notwithstanding the trouble he has caused me. I trust in God to bring us all through. It does not seem possible that we should have been preserved through so many perils, and such long-continued suffering, only to perish at last.

What happens in starvation? What happens when finally a body begins to feed on itself? First the fat deposits go, then the muscles, then the organs. The intestines begin to break down and diarrhea results. The blood pressure falls and the pulse weakens. Edema—an excess of watery fluids in the cavities or tissues—can occur. Life-threatening infections such as pneumonia or tuberculosis can set in.

Once more, Tyson feared cannibalism—and the disgrace that such a crime would bring. "Some of the men have dangerous looks; this hunger is disturbing their brains," he reported. To the Inuit, such fear was based on historical reality and family tragedy. In 1835, a sister of Tookoolito's had been part of a group of three boat crews who perished by starvation after resorting to cannibalism. They had been on their way from Cumberland Sound to Igloolik when overcome by misfortunes.

Just below the captives was all that noise. It might be Sedna throwing chunks of ice. It might be her dog, howling. It might be the storms of eternal damnation. The passageway to the next life was rumbling and close. It might open and swallow them at any moment.

Meyer looked increasingly bad, and some of the men's heads and faces were swollen. Tyson said he did not know the cause of the swelling, but that it definitely was not scurvy. No diagnosis is possible from the few clues given, but one thing is certain: No matter how desperate conditions were, no members of the *Polaris* party ever suffered, at least to a serious degree, from scurvy, that most dreaded disease the sailors called "Herod's daughter." The raw meat they ate was a continuing antidote.

April 15 and 16 passed with calm conditions but temperatures down to as low as ten degrees below zero. Thick snow alternated with sun. A one-hour watch was set. The men were too weak to stay up longer. Again, there was pilfering. Someone had been stealing pemmican. In his notebook, Tyson recorded:

*Robert[,] William and Fred they have been the three Principle thieves of
the party. Robert was caught on the night of 7th of this month in the
act. . . . Cannibalism troubles me very much.*

On the same day, April 16, Herron also noted the renewed possibility of
cannibalism. "It is a fearful thought," he recorded, "but may as well be looked
boldly in the face as otherwise." By the next day, he expressed stronger emotions about the chief pilferer: "We shot the dogs last winter for stealing the
provisions. If I had my way, with the consent of all hands, I would call out
and shoot down that two-legged dog. . . ." But there was nothing to do but
lower the allowance once more. Most of the men by now had swollen faces
and all were very weak.

On the seventeenth, the latitude reached was 54°27' north. It was like
climbing down the rungs of a perilous ladder from a house on fire—but the
house was frozen and the ground below was a deep and stormy sea. There
may or may not be rescuers bobbing out there in the swells, waiting for them.
There was no way of knowing until the rescuers arrived—if they ever did.

Then, on the eighteenth, a miracle: Ebierbing worked his way over the
loose ice to a small hole he had discerned half a mile away and shot a seal.
He called for his kyack. It took an hour to get it to him, but it was delivered
in time. A good-sized seal, enough for three meals, was the reward for this
dangerous effort. The seal was carefully divided, then distributed in the traditional manner that prevented bias: A man with his back to the meat
handed out the portions as each person's name was called.

Once more there was raw seal meat and blood and the energy it im-
parted. (Inuit said the sooner—and warmer—the meat was eaten, the more
energy it provided.) And now, too, there was the joyful sight of land: the
west coast. Though it quickly disappeared in snow and fog, there was no
mistake: It was there. For extra assurance, a large flock of ducks and a raven,
as well as other land birds, flew over them.

They had meat, and land was in sight. They were also down to their last
few pounds of pemmican and bread, just enough for tonight. And, by night-
fall, the breeze was up, and the swell, that harbinger of storm.

The next night, April 20, the party was flung into an all-out battle for
their lives. At nine, the watch cried out, but already a deadly wave was
sweeping across their piece of ice, devouring everything that was not secure.

Wave after wave struck, with an interval of five to ten minutes between. Finally, a monstrous wave hit, taking with it the tent, skins, and most of the bedding. The only things that were saved had already been stashed in the boat with the women and children; and there is little chance that the children would have survived if not already protected.

There was only one hope and task now—to save the boat; it had become their world. Every man was to hold it with all his remaining strength. If they failed, they were doomed. Tyson barked the orders, the only words of the night: "Hold on, my hearties! Bear down on her! Put on all your weight!" They tried to tie the boat to nearby projecting pieces of ice, but there were no grapnels or ice anchors. The lines kept breaking free.

The scene was almost unimaginable: As wild seas broke over them, the twelve men clung to their boat with an energy born of desperation. Wave after wave knocked them off their feet onto the ice, but they would not let go, even as the wind pushed the boat further and further back to the opposite edge of the floe. They held on, as Herron commented, "like grim death."

Every time they were thrown back, Tyson insisted that they move the boat up to the front of the floe where the waves first hit; otherwise, the momentum of the waves sweeping over the ice would make their job impossible. The heaviest seas came in intervals of fifteen or twenty minutes, with cycles of lesser ones in between. Every so often the boat was lifted entirely off the ice, and the men with it, sometimes carried the entire length of the floe. But, with superhuman strength, the men pulled it back each time. The water that was breaking over them was not clear water. It was filled with blocks of ice, crashing against the men and sometimes—as Tyson said—knocking them over as if they were so many pins in a bowling alley. Some blocks were as large as a chest of drawers.

Toward morning, Tookoolito and Mersek got out of the boat in which they had huddled with the children all night and worked with the men to hold it. Meyer had no strength at all. He could barely hang on to keep himself from being washed away. And so the desperate night passed. The battle raged from 9:00 P.M. until 7:00 A.M.

At dawn, a fragment of ice floated by. Tyson decided they must reach it. As dangerous as the effort was, there was really no choice. The scrap they were on could not last. And so he ordered, "Launch away!" and they did, scrambling aboard the boat. Jackson fell overboard but was rescued. They soon made their way to the new piece of ice, climbed onto it, ate a few bites of what food was left, then lay down in their wet clothes to rest. Except for deep bruises from the flying blocks of ice, everyone appeared as well as could be.

There were no dry clothes nor any means of getting dry. There was little sun. Still, the refugees took off all the clothes they could in order to attempt to dry them.

Life now consisted of trying to sleep and watching. Two days after claiming their new floe, the weather turned bad again. The soft, "pashy" ice, as Tyson called it, was thickening and hardening; to seek seals by foot or by ky-ack was impossible.

There was no food left. Meyer was close to the last stages of starvation. The party, exhausted from their efforts of two nights before, were very much weakened. They had to get some nourishment. They tried eating some dried skin, saved for clothing, that had been thrown into the boat when the storm began. Tyson, always ready to call on his faith, was confident of divine intervention. Ebierbing, always ready to try again, ventured out onto the soft ice once, twice, three times. On the fourth trip out, he came back hurriedly. He had seen a bear! All the party were ordered to lie down, in imitation of seals, and keep still, while Ebierbing climbed up on a hummock and Hans crouched down behind it. The bear came on slowly, duped by the plan. He thought he was coming for a seal dinner. Suddenly, both hunters fired, and the bear fell dead. The party arose with a shout. There was food! Everyone rushed to the body and helped to drag it back to "camp."

The blood was especially appreciated, because thirst was now as big a problem as hunger. Once they cut into the bear, they found that his stomach was empty. He was farther south than he was meant to be, and he was thin and hungry—an animal, like them, caught in the wrong range, trapped be-yond his limits, carried by all-powerful currents. But all the better, Tyson noted. His flesh was not permeated with the fat that creates strong taste. In every way, he was truly the miracle bear. Meyer made a quick recovery.

For the next two days the party drifted, red with blood, soaked with rain and sea water. Two large flocks of ducks flew over, and every so often there was a glimpse of land to the west. Leads opened but always closed before they could launch the boat. And the boat was a near wreck, with no means of repair.

Once more, on the morning of April 25, a gale kicked up the sea to such an extent that escape from their diminishing plate of ice became mandatory. It almost seemed a toss-up: Which would founder first, the boat or the ice-raft? But the answer was fairly clear. Knowing their only real hope was the boat, they took it and pushed off. For eight hours they struggled, attempting to row westward. They made no movement to the west but did secure another piece of ice and hauled up on it for the night. There was heavy snow—no sun—and no way of taking an observation. They could not figure how far they had drifted or where they were.

A gale and heavy sea challenged them throughout the night of April 27–28. With water washing over the floe, the group had to stand "all ready" by the boat. Conditions, however, were not so severe as on the night of April 20. At daylight, they launched the boat but could make no headway. After an hour of fighting into a gale, they hauled up on another fragment, lay down, and slept on the ice.

Shortly after noon, it was clear that they were threatened by a number of icebergs. Crashing and smashing—appearing to be fighting among themselves—the bergs bore down on them with horrific noise. With the roar of wind and wave as well, it was a cacophony of terror. Tyson called the watch and, at 1:00 P.M., launched the boat once more.

With water opening before them, they moved on. Ebierbing shot three young bladder-nose seals which, since they were small, were hauled into the boat. The dispossessed continued on, finding their way west through the opening ice, eating raw seal, drinking the blood that gave them energy and quenched their thirst.

Then, at 4:30 P.M., the miracle, the fantasy: a *steamer* ahead, to the north! Scrambling, the party hoisted its colors and pulled toward her. She appeared to be working her way southwest through the ice. But then she was gone.

The group was despondent. They boarded yet another shard of ice, once more hauled up the boat and made camp. The night was clear with a new moon and stars brightly shining—the first they had seen for a week. The sea was quiet and they could rest. They took the blubber of the three young seals and built fires on the floe to attract any vessel that might pass by in the night.

Two watches of four hours were set. Hope now kept the party wakeful just as fear had in the past few days, for now they were watching for rescue, not rogue waves.

In arctic annals, rescue comes in many forms. Sometimes it is of large dimensions, such as the case of the Dutch Greenland fleet in the late summer of 1777. Nine ships were wrecked in the ice, with combined crews of between 300 and 400 men. After several weeks on the ice, with little food and clothing, the party divided. One group, of about 200, reached land and attempted to struggle south. They all perished. The second group remained on the ice until it drifted south to a point where they could reach shore by boat. There, they received help from native Greenlanders, who enabled them to reach a Danish settlement. About 140 men survived.

Sometimes rescue is of a small and personal nature, such as happened with five crew members separated from the Scottish whaler *Horticula* in the fogs of Melville Bay. Peter Freuchen's wife Navarana first spotted the strangers many miles away on Saunders Island. Freuchen organized a group to cross the ice-choked water from Thule to meet them. When he arrived at their camp, one of the crew said:

"I am glad to see that there are other people in the world than the five of us," . . . and burst out laughing. The sound seemed loud and strange, and the man became embarrassed. He calmed down until suddenly his laughter turned into loud sobbing, and tears were running down his cheeks.

Rescue can also come to the solitary and truly helpless. Ebierbing's uncle, Ugarng, had in his party a young man named Etu, who had been abandoned on an island as a child because of birth defects. He managed to sustain himself, by catching birds, until a group of hunters happened upon him and saved him.

It is all a question of the kindness of strangers.

On the morning of April 29, another steamer was sighted, about eight miles off. Tyson called the watch, launched the boat, and made for her. After an hour's pull they lost her and were once more beset in the ice.

Again, they landed on a chunk of ice. They hoisted their flag, climbed to the highest part of their island, and simultaneously fired three rounds from their rifles and pistols. Then—a response of three shots! The steamer headed toward them. Deliverance was at hand.

But the steamer changed course, heading south, then north, then west.

She got no closer. She worked at it all day but apparently was unable to make her way through the ice. Late in the afternoon she steamed away, heading southwest. The *Polaris* group gave up. In the evening, she reappeared, but farther away.

As the party searched after the first steamer, a second hove into sight, on the other side.

At sunset, land was visible to the southwest, about thirty-five miles distant. Meyer claimed they were at latitude 49° north, but Tyson said they were not that far south. Tyson said it was 53°0'5" north. Hans caught a baby seal, the smallest taken aboard so far.

At 5:00 A.M. on April 30, came a cry from the lookout on watch: "There's a steamer! There's a steamer!" Tyson, resting in the boat, sprang out and ordered all the guns to be fired while the group set up a simultaneous shout. The colors went up on the mast, and Tyson ordered Hans off in his kyack in order to intercept the ship in the fog.

The steamer, a quarter of a mile away, was headed right for them. In a few minutes, she was alongside the floe.

Tyson took off his old Russian cap, which he had worn all through the winter, and, waving it over his head, led the group in giving three cheers. A hundred men, lining the deck and rigging of the steamer, returned it. They were the crew of the *Tigress*, a barkentine out of Conception Bay, Newfoundland, under Captain Isaac Bartlett (an uncle of the famous Captain Robert "Bob" Bartlett of the *Karluk* and of Robert E. Peary's numerous attempts at the North Pole).

The men of the *Tigress* lowered boats, but the *Polaris* group, throwing everything out of their boat, quickly got theirs in the water. In the meantime, the *Tigress* crew bounded onto the floe, peering into the dirty pans that had been used over the fires—the only belongings left to these strange picnickers. The ice-drifters had been in the process of making soup out of the blood and entrails of the last small seal that Hans had shot.

On board, the party was immediately surrounded by their incredulous rescuers. They asked Tyson how long the party had been on the ice. When he answered, "Since the 15th of last October," they were dumbfounded. One crew member had to ask, "And was you on it night and day?" For the first time in all those months, Tyson experienced the strange sensation of laughing.

Captain Bartlett invited Tyson down into the cabin, where he got a pipe and tobacco. He then got a breakfast of cod and potatoes and hard bread and coffee—a meal he said he enjoyed more than any other in his life.

The latitude of the rescue, Tyson learned, was 53°35' north, off Grady Harbor, Labrador. The steamer they saw on the twenty-ninth was the *Eagle* of St. John's. Her captain had never seen them.

Undoubtedly the two Inuit families were welcomed by the sailors. Undoubtedly they were made comfortable and warm and were well fed. Undoubtedly they were treated with courtesy and compassion, and much made of the children. But Tyson was quit of them. He had done his job. Remarkably, he had delivered each of his charges to safety. All eighteen were alive and—for the most part—well. He was released from what must be the strangest of commands ever entered into upon the seven seas.

Tyson gave the battered *Polaris* boat to the captain's son. (Later, the boy injured his hand with the premature discharge of a Remington rifle brought on board by the party.)

It was now May, the Moon for the Birth of the Young Oogjook and the Musk Ox. The *Tigress* still had work to do. May 2 and 3, a violent gale, with unusually cold temperatures, battered the sealer. Captain Bartlett kept her headed west, out of the swell. He said it was the heaviest gale he had yet experienced this trip. The rescued knew they would not have survived this storm, certainly not where they were, right at the mouth of the open ocean. The gale continued into the following day, with the *Tigress* fast in the ice. May 5, the men—including Ebierbing—were out and killed 600 seals. When the ship worked its way to where the seals lay dead, however, they could collect fewer than half of them; the others had been taken by another sealer.

On May 7, Captain Bartlett decided to go home. Several of the men were sick, as were Tookoolito and Ebierbing. Both Meyer and Tyson were suffering from swollen feet and ankles. Meyer also had frozen hands. Since coming on board, the whole party was troubled, in one way or another, with colds, sore throats, and rheumatism. Captain Bartlett decided to cut thirty-five miles off the trip and put into Conception Bay instead of St. John's.

Soon after the *Tigress* anchored, the American consul of Harbor Grace came aboard, listened to the particulars of the ice floe party, and telegraphed them to the consul at St. John's: The story—which no one would at first believe—was now working its way south down the coast to Washington, D.C., to the Secretary of the Navy, and to President Grant.

When they arrived at St. John's on the night of May 12, there was a large crowd waiting to see them. They were heroes. Already, the publicity hounds were on their trail.

May 13, Harper & Brothers sent a telegram requesting a photograph for the *Weekly*. Secretary of the Navy Robeson also sent a telegram, ordering Tyson to take charge of the *Polaris* party on the passage home; he was not quite through after all. The Inuit families were besieged with well-wishers and the curious. Many knew of Tookoolito and Ebierbing through Hall's book, *Life with the Esquimaux*, published in 1864. Finally, Tyson had to prohibit visitors to the two families. The children were sick, at least in part from the cakes and candies given to them.

May 16 brought news that Secretary Robeson had ordered the U.S. steamship *Frolic* to pick up the party at St. John's and convey them to Washington. On June 5, 1873, they arrived—five days less than two years after the *Polaris* first sailed out of Washington with careful instructions to Commander Hall from Secretary Robeson.

In Cumberland Sound, June was known as the Moon for the Birth of the Young Deer and the Walrus. In Washington, it was now time for the government to sort out the confusion and tragedy of its first expedition to the North Pole.

From this point on, there are no more personal accounts of the *Polaris* ice floe survivors. The voices fade and scatter, their world blown apart like a handful of snow in a gale, dispersed in every direction.

Eventually, Captain Budington and the thirteen men who stayed aboard the *Polaris* would return to tell their tale. They were all alive and spoke their piece, but their story came with a sound like wind through frozen rigging. No one would ever quite be sure of what had been said.

Chapter Eleven

✳

4:00 P.M., June 5, 1873–Close of Business, December 26, 1873

THE NAVY INQUIRY: LETTING LOOSE THE GHOST

The burial of Captain Hall, Polaris Bay, November 10, 1871, 11:00 A.M.

I was returning to Washington, D.C., for further research before going on to visit my mother in New York. It was summer, July—a month after the time when Tookoolito and her family arrived on board the *Frolic*. For them, it would have been the Moon for the Birth of the Young Eider Duck.

The weather seemed unusually damp and cool. Moisture hung heavy in the air as I entered the Washington Navy Yard at Ninth and M Streets, close to where the *Periwinkle* had become the *Polaris* and sailed to the furthest northing and where her passengers had returned without her. I wondered what Tookoolito had felt—heat, undoubtedly, of an overwhelming nature, heat like a rogue wave that would not crest and break. And what of Mersek and her children, who had never been out of their snowy home? What was their reaction? What did they say, turning to Tookoolito, their only hope for interpretation?

At the Naval Historical Center, I entered the Navy Department Library. Established in 1800 by order of President John Adams, it is one of the few major military historical libraries open to the public and one of the original depository libraries. From the Navy's earliest signal book of 1797 to captured German submarine material of 1944, it contains a world of information. But I had only one aim—the photography section with its materials pertaining to the *Periwinkle/Polaris*.

What I found was a curious and curiously mixed collection including an image of Hall that looks unlike that of the one recognized photograph. It shows a balding man with short, light hair and moustache but no beard.

Also included is a photograph of a sketch of Hall's grave with the memorial erected by the Nares expedition of 1875. Most interesting are the sketches by Emil Schumann, chief engineer of the steam department on board the *Polaris*. These, showing the Greenland towns visited and the situation of the ship locked in the ice, provide an eye-witness account. Here, in Grandma Moses style, is the going-forth and the going-away of the *Polaris*, the funeral of Hall, and the Parting; here are seals and local people as they were seen in 1871. Although there was a camera on board, cold temperatures and condensation rendered it inoperable. But there was Emil Schumann with his pencil.

According to Tyson, Schumann "was a German, regularly educated for his profession, and a draughtsman of considerable skill." What Schumann said of himself was that he was born in Dresden, capital of Saxony, in 1843, and that he was an "engineer of bridge and road building and laying out streets, etc."

We can thank him for applying his skills—all of them—in a way that undoubtedly he never imagined. His sketches became the basis for numerous derivative illustrations. When all the words on the disaster have collided, intermingled, and dissolved like flakes of snow and charges and countercharges have blurred, these simple depictions remain: A tiny ship is trapped in ice; minute figures walk across an endless, dismal terrain; they bury their commander; they separate. These sketches define the territory of truth. In lieu of mechanical means, they stand as evidence.

The Navy lost no time in investigating what had happened aboard the *Polaris* and sending its findings to President Grant. As we look back from our hurried electronic age, it is remarkable to see just how quickly this happened. The *Report to the President of the United States of the Action of the Navy Department in the matter of the disaster to the United States exploring expedition toward the north pole, accompanied by a report of the examination of the rescued party, etc.* is dated June 17, 1873. It encompasses an examination begun twelve days earlier—at 4 P.M. on Thursday, June 5—of every member of the ice floe party except for Mersek, who spoke no English, and the five children. The examination was completed in six days and published almost immediately. The thirteen personal statements, taken down in shorthand, are accompanied by the diaries of two men who rode the ice—Frederick Meyer and John Herron—as well as those of two men who stayed behind on the *Polaris*—William Morton and Herman Siemans. These last two journals had been thrown overboard onto the ice in the confusion of the night of October 15. Siemans's, written in German, was picked up by Robert Kruger; Morton's—one page—was picked up by William Jackson and handed over to Kruger, who saved them both.

Attached to the report, and set before the testimony, is a copy of Hall's last dispatch, dated Sixth Snow House Encampment, Cape Brevoort, North Side Entrance to Newman's Bay, latitude 82°3' north, longitude 61°20' west, October 20, 1871. It was found among his personal papers in his writing desk, which Ebierbing preserved throughout the adventure on the ice and delivered personally to Robeson.

A copy of the dispatch was carefully buried, as was customary, in a disguised cairn "on the brow of the second plain from the sea, about fifty feet above its level." Ebierbing dug the hole. The paper was placed in an air- and water-tight copper cylinder sealed with white beeswax. It was further protected by pieces of board from a twenty-eight-pound wooden box that Hall had ordered to be taken apart the previous night. One was marked "10 F. E." This and thirteen other pieces of the box were scattered within a monument of stones two feet high and two-and-a-half feet long at the base. A piece of slate marked similarly was placed under the lettered board in a hole.

An untutored marauder would find nothing but these pieces of board and slate, the strange lettering, and an otherwise empty hole. A knowledgeable searcher would understand the code to read, Look "10 feet to the east."

And there, in an otherwise unmarked spot, the message to the Honorable Secretary of the United States Navy lay buried. It was written on a form used for such correspondence. In English and five other languages, the bearer is asked:

> *Whoever finds this paper is requested to forward it to the Secretary of the Navy, Washington, D.C., with a note of the time and place at which it was found; or, if more convenient, to deliver it for that purpose, to the U.S. Consul at the nearest port.*

The copy of the 1873 report to the President I obtained, through interlibrary loan, came from the Smithsonian. I was charged $1.60. It is a thin hardbound book of small typeface and 154 pages printed by the U.S. Government Printing Office. It is falling apart. Indeed, the strings of the binding gave way as I handled it, the sheets pulling free, breaking away from the center: All seeks to move out into space, finding its own trajectory. Maybe the next person who requests the report will not be able to obtain this copy and will not be able to read its words. Perhaps that person will not search further. The path wears smooth, the tracks fill in, the signs become illegible.

The well-credentialed inquiry examiners included Robeson, Secretary of the Navy; Commodore William Reynolds, senior officer of the Navy Department; Professor Spencer F. Baird of the Smithsonian; Captain H. W. Howgate of the Army signal service (which had employed Meyer and detailed him over to the *Polaris*). They convened aboard the U.S. steamship *Tallapoosa*.

In his introduction to the report, Robeson makes a strong statement that, while much that is said about Budington is negative, it is better to let the record stand than to suppress it and cause "sensational and alarming" reports. (Budington was still missing, along with the other thirteen men who had remained aboard the *Polaris*. Robeson had already given preparatory orders to the U.S. steamer *Juniata* to proceed to Greenland to start the search for them.) Of Budington's character, Robeson summed up:

> *The facts show that though he was perhaps wanting in enthusiasm for the grand objects of the expedition, and at times grossly lax in discipline, and though he differed in judgment from others as to the possibility, safety, and*

propriety of taking the ship farther north, yet he is an experienced and care-
ful navigator, and when not affected by liquor, of which there remained
none on board at the time of the separation, a competent and safe com-
mander.

Starting at 4:00 P.M. on Thursday, June 5, Tyson was examined. He was followed the next day, at 2:10 P.M., by Meyer. After him came Ebierbing, followed by Tookoolito. Then, Hans was questioned, followed by John Herron, Robert Kruger, Frederick Jamka, Gustavus Lindquist, William Linderman, Peter Johnson, Frederick Aunting, and William Jackson. Siemans's translated diary fills up pages 91 to 120. Morton's diary takes one page—121—and Meyer's the next twelve. Herron's diary fills the remainder of the text. Of the 154 pages, only 89 are testimony, mostly Tyson's and Meyer's.

What do they say?

The questioning centers on Hall's delirium and death and on Budington's actions. The examiners (we do not know who asked which questions or in what manner) probe the possibility of criminal action, but they probe gently indeed—remarkably so by our hardened standards. They are dealing with civilians, not military officers, and with an expedition, which, though officially under military command, was really a private enterprise created by political pressure; there was no official presence on board. The interviewers are both responsible and not responsible. The interrogations are designed to do what, on the surface, would be expected—but nothing more.

Both Tyson and Meyer testify to Budington's drinking as well as to his lack of effective leadership, to his dislike of Hall and his unwillingness to proceed north after Hall's death, even when he had a fair chance. Both speak firmly of how, after breaking away, they expected the *Polaris* to come for them; she was strong enough and could have gotten through the ice. In spite of all their difficulties during the drift, the two men seem curiously united in testimony. Their tones are different—Tyson's far more acrimonious—but the content of their answers is similar. Their tandem comments make for a damning portrait of the missing sailing master.

Given Tyson's bitter view of Budington, it is surprising that his comments are as restrained as they are. While on the ice, Tyson did not curtail his criticism of the captain: Beast, Villain, Base man, Liar, Coward, Thief, Glutton, Low Drunkard. Later, in his autobiographical statement, he took up the same tirade: "Budington I Brand as Low Villain. . . ." As a prisoner of the elements, considering Budington responsible for all the evil that had befallen the *Polaris* and her crew, he had longed to tell the truth and vanquish his enemy. Why did he hold back now when he had the chance? Clearly, though brave at sea, Tyson was not brave in the face of onshore authorities. From humble beginnings, he lacked the self-assurance of formal education and social status; though he lived within its domain, he was never part of the whaling establishment. He needed a job and feared what would happen if he made trouble. (Indeed, Tyson's career was to fizzle out. After leading Captain Howgate's preliminary and unsuccessful expedition to Cumberland Sound in 1877–78, he would go on to become a laborer and a messenger for the War Department; and the financial failure of his book canceled other hopes.)

The inquiry is not a court-martial. It is not even a civil judicial proceeding, nor are there rubrics to tell us precisely how the process was managed. There is no reference to the taking of an oath, no mention of whether witnesses were sequestered or were able to listen to one another. There is no consistent form of questioning. Witnesses were encouraged to give their own narrative, taking their testimony where they chose. Much of the information given is technical, not personal, and veers off on tangents. There is no cross-examination.

And, of course, there is no Budington to defend himself.

What of Tookoolito?

Tookoolito, the expedition's interpreter, is given two pages and nine lines. She answers questions about Hall's death. She did not think he was poisoned.

> *Question. Did he tell you anything about his papers?*
> *Answer. O, yes. He said to take care of the papers; get them home, and give them to the Secretary [of the Navy]. If anything had happened to the Secretary, to give them to some one else. After his death I told Captain Buddington [sic] of this charge several times. He said he would give them to me by and by.*

Her final words:

Question. Who was in command of the party on the ice?
Answer. Nobody.
Question. Was not Captain Tyson in command?
Answer. Well, he did not have much. He could not control them. He tried to do everything he could. He was a good man. We have known him a good many years. He tried to do everything for the best; sometimes they would not mind him; I sorry, and Joe very sorry too. . . .

Hans gets half a page, which concludes:

Hannah (Tookoolito) was directed to ask Hans if he had anything more to say. [Hannah.] He has nothing further he wants to say. Too hot here; children sick, and he wants to go home right off.
[Hans much pleased at promise of return to Greenland.]

The gentle steward, John Herron, was the only one Tyson excepted from the group he disparaged as "the men" or "the Germans." He was also a person who had nothing in particular at stake—no professional reputation, no unusual ambitions, and no personal ties with the principals. When questioned why the *Polaris* did not come for them, he generously answered:

. . . I don't think Captain Buddington meant to abandon us. He either thought we could easily get ashore, or else he could not get through the ice. I don't think he would do anything of the kind. Standing on the ship, you would naturally think we could get ashore; it may have looked to him that we were right under the lee of the shore. It is very likely that he thought we could get ashore, and that he didn't understand our signals.

Did Budington have a hand in the death of Hall? We may never know, but Prussian seaman Frederick Jamka's testimony was chilling in its implications:

. . . He [Hall] died either at midnight or early in the morning. One of the men went aft in the morning and met Captain Buddington. The captain said, "Well, Henry [Hobby], there is a stone off my heart." Henry said, "Why so?" "Why, Captain Hall is dead." We did not like that very well. . . .

And what of the *Polaris* and the fourteen men who stayed aboard her and who appeared to have abandoned their nineteen cohorts severed from them on the night of the Separation? What had become of them?

According to an account by Rear Admiral C. H. Davis, the *Polaris* held together through the storm that tore apart her company. On board after the Separation, it was found that the ship was in young ice five miles from the coast. The first mate went to the crow's nest to search for the missing party; he saw no sign of life but possibly some provisions on a floe in the middle of the strait. (Others said it was black ice, stones, or debris.) Another crew member searched from the crow's nest as well. At 8:00 A.M., leads of water opened up toward the shore. Captain Budington decided to take advantage of these openings and get the stricken ship to land as soon as possible. Once there, she was secured to large grounded hummocks of ice, lying on her starboard side toward the beach, 400 yards away. They named the spot Life-Boat Cove. Providentially, they had come to rest near the settlement of Etah, whose residents would save them from scurvy and starvation.

Early on the morning of October 17, the crew was put to work preparing to abandon ship. On the nineteenth, the first visitors from Etah arrived. Later, they returned with help, to complete getting the supplies off the ship and onto shore, where a building—"Polaris House"—was being constructed. The visiting Inuit were particularly surprised by the ship's cat and by the live lemmings being kept as specimens and as pets: According to the fireman W. F. Campbell, who had brought the cat from Washington, the Inuit guests "had never seen a cat before and were very much interested in it. They gave it the name we called it by, 'Tommy.' They have a name for it in the Esquimaux language, though they have not the animal itself."

On the twenty-fourth, with everything useful carried to the upper deck, the pump was allowed to stop: The *Polaris* had been taken off life support.

By the twenty-sixth, the water inside had risen to within three feet of the upper deck. A gale blew. Comfortable in their new, well-supplied quarters ashore, the men wondered if their lost companions were exposed to the storm. The consensus was, Tyson had led the group to land, somewhere to the south, and would travel up the coast to meet them at any time.

As the days went by, various side trips were made. The first mate went off with an Inuit family on a caribou hunt. A party was sent out to look for a boat left nearby by the Hayes expedition of 1860. No trace was found. Various hunting trips were made; occasional foxes were secured. The people of Etah were starving. But in Polaris House there were nights of fiddling, singing, and merriment. On election day, the crew voted for President of the United States.

By December, the coffee was gone and rye was used in its place. Sad stories of want emerged from Etah, where dogs were being killed for food, and from where, during the winter, emissaries would come begging.

The memory of the missing ice floe group hung heavy in the atmosphere. Still, a regular routine was entered into: breakfast at nine; a morning of observations, journal-writing, cleaning firearms, etc.; dinner at three o'clock; chess, checkers, dominoes, and cards in the evening; bed at ten. The shy cat, Tommy, stayed in the captain's bunk by day and frolicked through the house at night.

During January, preparations began to be made to build two small boats out of the wreck of the *Polaris* and make an escape from Life-Boat Cove. What was not going to be used for the boats was used for firewood. By February, the sun began to reappear. A raven visited, and a window was made in the roof of the house in order to cut down on the need for lamps. As the weather warmed, visits and various side trips continued. During one such exploration, the despoiled grave of Sonntag, his bones scattered, was found and repaired.

On May 30, as final preparations for departure were being made, the *Polaris* went adrift. She was carried about 200 yards toward the south, where she again grounded. At high tide her upper deck was two feet below the surface of the water.

June 2, Hall's arctic library was cached, along with the pendulum, the transit instrument without its glasses, three box chronometers, the two log books of the *Polaris,* and a statement of accomplishment and the prospect of rescue.

On the third, the two boats were launched—one under the command of Captain Budington and one under the command of First Mate Chester—and made their way slowly, and with much difficulty, down the icy coast. On the morning of the seventh, after a storm, and during onshore repairs to Captain Budington's boat on Hakluyt Island, a member of the party was lost: Tommy the cat, which "had become quite wild from the excitement of the journey and its confined quarters . . . ran away, disappeared among the rocks and was not again seen."

If the cat had remained calm, it would have soon known relief. Early on the morning of June 23, Chester shouted, "Ship ahoy!" It was the *Ravenscraig* of Kirkcaldy, Scotland, which found them in latitude 75°38' north, longitude 65°35' west and took them aboard with every kindness and consideration. But, of course, there were no communications beyond the ice.

It would be months—the entire summer, the summer of the inquiry— before the Navy learned of the fate of the men of the *Polaris*. In the meantime, it set out to find them. And again, it wasted no time.

The search for the missing *Polaris* had a dreamlike quality. Like so many cases in arctic history, it was a quest in which the searchers and searched-for were strangely interwoven, their pasts interconnected, their themes similar, sometimes their names changed as if in disguise: an opera of subplots and arias held together by a haunting motif and bound to reach a dramatic dénouement.

The *Tigress*, rescuer of the floe captives, was chartered and refitted for the search mission. In the meantime, the available but ill-equipped *Juniata* set sail from New York on June 24, under Commander D. L. Braine. Her ice pilot was none other than James Monroe Budington, uncle of the missing Captain Sydney O. Budington and former adversary of George E. Tyson. Her steam launch, the *Little Juniata*, was under the command of Lieutenant George Washington De Long—a man who would later achieve posthumous fame in the disastrous wreck of the *Jeannette* in the ice north of Siberia in 1881. (When pieces of the *Jeannette* were found three years later on the southwest coast of Greenland, De Long's theory was proved: The arctic currents flow clockwise around the pole. Even more curiously, before her name was changed, the *Jeannette* used to be the *Pandora*, on which Ebierbing had served under the previous owner.) The *Juniata* and her launch were to provide logistical support for the main search vessel, the *Tigress*, which, when made ready, set sail from New York on July 14. James A. Greer was the commander. Also on board the *Tigress* was George E. Tyson, Acting Lieutenant, serving as ice master.

Now there were two ice masters—Tyson and James Budington—sailing tandem in the same expedition in search of the missing captain whom they sought with such very different motives. Irony walked the rolling decks. The two rivals had last seen each other when the supply ship *Congress* pulled away from the *Polaris* at Godhavn on August 17, 1871.

Also on board the *Tigress* were Ebierbing, who had been hired as interpreter, and Hans and Hans's family, who were going home. As if haunted, Tyson was also accompanied by three other floe-drifters: his nemesis, Kruger, along with Lindquist and Linderman. Yet others, who had agreed to return to the scene of their grief, failed to appear when the *Tigress* set sail. Enlivening the stormy passage was Frank V. Commagere, yeoman, who was, in reality, a reporter for *The New York Herald*.

By now, the story of the *Polaris* and her castaways was famous. Thousands saluted the *Tigress* as she steamed toward Long Island Sound—a far more lively send-off than the *Polaris* had experienced two years earlier.

On August 14, the *Tigress* reached the point of separation—Littleton Island and nearby McGary Island—and the deserted *Polaris* camp at Life-Boat Cove. But it wasn't deserted. Four or five visitors from Etah continued on, some dressed in the abandoned clothes of their former hosts. A confusion of supplies was found scattered about, with no sign of effort to seal and protect records, books, or scientific instruments. A logbook was discovered with all reference to the death of Captain Hall ripped out.

After a severe gale and much damage on board, the *Tigress* made fast in Cumberland Sound on September 4. Tyson noted: "This seems like home— it is my old whaling-ground, and here we are, snug and comfortable, in Niountelik Harbor, so familiar to me." This was Tookoolito and Ebierbing's Niantilik. There, Tyson met some of his, and Hall's, old friends and took note of the many deaths that had occurred. He feared the people of Cumberland Sound would soon be extinct.

The voyage of the *Tigress* was marked with pummeling storms, and many of the frightened crew became sick. On October 16, as she entered St. John's Harbor, the pilot gave the word, "The *Polaris* party are safe." With that happy news, the battered vessel continued on her way, reaching New York on November 10. Almost a month earlier, on September 18—the day the news was telegraphed from Scotland—the *Juniata* had been flagged down as she set out to sea again from St. John's with orders to continue the mission of discovering the fate of the *Polaris*.

While the search by the *Juniata* and the *Tigress* was in progress, the objects of the search—the fourteen missing men—were comfortably cruising the northern waters. As surprise guests aboard an arctic whaler on duty, they were compelled to follow, with their hosts, the vagaries of fish and weather. July passed in the ice, as the *Ravenscraig* tortuously worked her way across Baffin Bay, to the west. Having entered Lancaster Sound on July 6, she then crossed to Admiralty Inlet. There she met the steamer *Arctic*, whose captain agreed to take on half the *Polaris* men: Chester, Bessels, Schumann, Hayes, Siemens, Hobby, and Campbell. Ten days later, the steamer *Intrepid* took on Bryan, Mauch, and Booth. On August 20, the four remaining men—Budington, Morton, Odell, and Coffin—transferred to the *Arctic*, which proceeded home. She reached Dundee, Scotland, on September 18. The long-traveling passengers arrived in New York on October 7. On September 13, the *Intrepid* passengers—Bryan, Mauch, and Booth—transferred to the *Eric*, and, after a perilous voyage, reached Dundee on October 22. Mauch and Booth left from Glasgow on the twenty-fourth and arrived in New York on November 7. Bryan, who traveled to Edinburgh, London, Paris, and Dublin, arrived in New York on November 13.

The kindness of these whaling strangers was officially noted and compensated. The Navy awarded to the owners of the four rescue ships payment for the subsistence they provided. Captain Allen of the *Ravenscraig* received $800; the owners, $500; and each of the men who walked the ice to rescue the party, $25. The captains of the other ships—including Bartlett of the *Tigress*—received $300 each. The captain of each vessel was also invited "to purchase a gold pocket chronometer, and to have inscribed thereon that it was 'a token of the gratitude of the United States for kindness to the officers and men of the *Polaris*.'"

The men were duly questioned upon their return to the United States: Budington, Chester, Morton, Bessels, Schumann, Odell, Coffin, Campbell, Siemens, Hobby, and Hayes on October 11; and Bryan, Mauch, and Booth on December 24, with an adjournment until December 26. Again, the sessions were held on board the *Tallapoosa*. The information from these examinations did not, as Davis notes, "in any manner, qualify or change the report of the Secretary, of June 16th."

Again, the prime subject was Budington. This time the sailing master was present but hardly his best defense. He admitted to most of the charges made but claimed he was never incapacitated by alcohol. When asked if any of Hall's papers had been burned, Budington answered:

> *At one time during his sickness we were having a talk together about one thing and another. He said he had written a letter to me and took it out, and he thought I had better not see it; but if I insisted, he would show it to me. I told him it didn't make any odds. He then said he thought it ought to be burned, as he did not approve of it, and he held it to the candle and burned it. He said he thought I had better not see it, and therefore he burned it. This was between his first and last sickness, and during his lucid intervals. No other part of the journal, or anything else, was burned at any time, to my knowledge.*

According to subsequent testimony, a box containing Hall's papers was apparently put onto the ice floe on the night of October 15 and disappeared in the stormy chaos of the Separation. We would never learn from the commander's hand what happened—or what he thought had happened—during his final days on board the *Polaris.*

The interrogators plodded on, attempting to reconstruct the mysterious events, but the darkness could not—or would not—be plumbed. They officially concurred with the report of Dr. Bessels: Hall had died of apoplexy, or a stroke. It was not a report to be proud of. They ordered a limited number to be printed.

The Navy had done all it was going to do. Its *Polaris* expedition, though ending in disaster, had achieved certain goals: the furthest northing, discovery of previously unknown geography, and the laying to rest of the myth of the Open Polar Sea. More than 700 miles of coastline were discovered and reconnoitered. Facts and specimens of magnetism, meteorology, mineralogy, hydrology, geology, botany, and zoology were compiled. Eight species of mammals, twenty-three of birds, fifteen of insects, and seventeen of plants were found. The commander's death was explained. The bills were paid. The survivors went away, along with the reporters and sensation-seekers. Only the questions remained, centered on the specter of Hall in his farthest-north grave, an arctic willow growing over what once had been his heart.

Chapter Twelve

June 16, 1873–December 31, 1876

GROTON: THE FINAL YEARS

Groton, Connecticut, 1870s

In Washington, I was still trying to find Punny's story. It should not have been so difficult, but nowhere could I find a clear statement. Hall had failed me, and I felt deeply disappointed.

As I walked through Union Station, I felt particularly close to Tookoolito. After the conclusion of the testimony on board the *Tallapoosa*, she had traveled north with Punny. This magnificent station did not exist then—it was completed in 1908, refurbished eighty years later—but I could imagine her waiting to board a train, holding the hand of her child, all that was left: Hurried, hot crowds pushed by them. Steam and noise enveloped them. Now they were truly on their own. Father Hall was gone. Tyson was gone and the *Polaris*.

Home had become a small house on Pleasant Valley Road in Groton, Connecticut, where she and Ebierbing had established themselves after the second trip with Hall. It was close to the farmhouse of the Budingtons, where they had spent considerable time.

I was going there now, to that conjunction of the Budingtons and the Baffin Islanders—that place once serendipitously called the Pleasant Valley Four Corners.

The Amtrak route along the waters of Long Island Sound is still quite lovely, in spite of development. I could look out, past the shore, to the sea route of the *Polaris* on her way to New London, and the route of the *Tigress*, her doppelgänger.

The train has been coming to New London since 1849. Only the station is different, the previous two having burned down. When Tookoolito arrived, New London was the whaling center for southern New England, rivaling New Bedford to the north. In 1876, it became the home of the U.S. Coast Guard Academy.

New London's sister city, Groton, was, in 1781, the site of a massacre of Colonial defenders by British troops under Benedict Arnold. In Tookoolito's time, it was a flat, spread-out town. Now, it is densely compacted: Site of the Electric Boat division of General Dynamics, it is known as the submarine capital of the world.

Here, the word "Polaris" is ubiquitous, but it has nothing to do with the *Polaris* that steamed into port on the morning of June 30, 1871, headed for the North Star. It refers to a nuclear ballistic missile and the submarine that carries it. "Polaris" submarines, which came into use during the 1960s, changed the nature of naval warfare. With the capability of launching nuclear missiles from beneath the water's surface, they provided an enormously expanded scope. Their targets were no longer simply other ships but now inland sites as well. With a range of 1,300 miles, they were able to stay on patrol for sixty days.

Forty-one "Polaris" submarines were built for the American Navy, while they also became major marine weapons for Great Britain, France, and the Soviet Union. They were succeeded by the Skipjack, Los Angeles, and Ohio classes carrying the newer, more intelligent Poseidon and Trident missiles and able to stay under water even longer. Since the *Nautilus* crossed the center of the North Pole on August 3, 1958, atomic-powered submarines—the new steel whales of the ocean—have regularly traveled under the ice cap; and sometimes they have fallen to the ocean floor with their drowned crews and their deadly cargos.

The evolution of the name "Polaris" indicates the difficulty of tracking truth. Not only has the name of the ship and its purpose changed dramatically, but the star itself has shifted position. Already, with the precession of the Earth's axis, it has drifted away from the Pole; within several hundred years it will no longer be the pole star exemplifying steadfastness in the universe. And now the two polar ice caps change in a fundamental way. As Earth warms, they melt and shrink, posing, perhaps, the greatest environmental hazard of all. In Antarctica, ice shelves as large as Connecticut have broken away, disintegrating into shipping lanes. In the Arctic, sea ice has thinned by 40 percent in the last thirty years. To the south, penguins wash ashore on Brazilian beaches. To the north, polar bears are struggling to find prey in their diminishing habitat. Melting ice moves currents that move weather; once mild areas could now quickly become cold, incurring a new ice age.

Sea water and blood are of a similar composition. Earth and the human body are composed of 70 percent water. For both, even the slightest elevation can bring disaster. An island—or a person—can be easily drowned.

If you want to learn what happened to Tookoolito and her family after the ice drift, you have to go to a place you might not easily discover without the assistance of helpful people: The Indian & Colonial Research Center on Main Street in Old Mystic, Connecticut. There, in a small building that looks as if it might once have been a church or a schoolhouse but was actually a bank, resides a loosely woven nest of clues: a scattering of letters, some semiofficial; a clutch of photographs, posed in studios and now badly faded; notes and notebooks; strange artifacts such as a bit of lace made by Tookoolito and a pistol with shoulder extension belonging to Ebierbing; and occasional newspaper articles, trailing off in the late 1930s as the last eyewitnesses shared their memories before leaving the scene.

During Tookoolito's Groton years, there was no zealous explorer nor dedicated journalist at her side prodding and recording. There was kindness, yes, but no field of energy surrounding her—politeness but no passion. And the politeness, undoubtedly, arose from both pity and Christian piety: Here were a woman and child from savage lands—alone and in need of charity and instruction—souls to be saved. No one was concerned with documenting the mundane existence of these Christians-in-training. Although she had once been a well-known traveler, an exotic, Tookoolito, now blown off course, was merely Hannah, a Connecticut housewife. Fortunately, there was just enough of a chain of community memory and caring to hold together a tiny collection of ephemera, a tenuous memorial.

Part of the chain of caring resided in a Mr. John Joseph Copp (1840–1914), a quiet and studious man who gave up the practice of law to manage his farm on Pleasant Valley Road. At one time he had power of attorney over Tookoolito and Ebierbing's nearby home. He collected photographs of the Baffin Islanders, which he donated to what is now known as the Monument House Museum at Fort Griswold Battlefield State Park; they continue to reside there. He took the time to write a history of Punny and note some reminiscences. He explained her adoption and said Hall brought it about by offering her father a sled, then added some shirts and knives to the "generous price already paid." When the time came for Tookoolito and Punny to leave their Groton home to join the *Polaris* expedition, it was he who drove them by carriage to meet the ferry to New York—an occasion of sadness for Tookoolito but one of exuberant excitement for the young child: She was going to be reunited with Grandpa Hall. Copp is just the kind of neighbor you would hope to find, especially if you had come from afar. As with his crops, he tended friendships well; in the case of Tookoolito and Punny, he helped keep their story alive.

Others in the chain of caring produced bits of information, while yet others brought them to the Research Center in Old Mystic and maintained them there. Some of this material is accurate, some not; much is sentimental. All was handed over to me.

For a researcher, there is more excitement in such a place than, say, the National Archives and Records Administration, where much is housed but all is carefully regulated, where guards and patrolling employees control the sense of wonder. And sure enough, while I worked with the director and her assistant on Main Street, the wonderful occurred: A hidden file of thirty Tookoolito letters—a file not seen for years—appeared, bringing sudden connection with the past. Many of these letters are from Tookoolito to "Mother" Budington. All help, in some way, to clarify the path: a gift.

Once—and it still seems remarkable within my family—I had a cousin who was murdered. Her father spared no expense in hiring private detectives to track and target the murderer, whose identity he claimed to know. But they did not start until twenty-four hours after the killing. After twenty-four hours, I clearly remember being told, the trail is cold. I was a child but could not forget. Daphne's death was never solved and avenged. And what now, after all these years? We can never know who, if anyone, murdered Hall, and we can never know exactly what happened to Tookoolito, whose loyal friendship to Hall had brought her back to this, his starting point. But these letters and personal comments—some hardly legible—help to explain how the two had come to switch places.

What we can piece together is this: First, before settling down in Groton, Tookoolito and Punny made a trip to Wiscasset, on the south coast of Maine, to visit their friends, the Baileys. In November, Ebierbing returned from the voyage of the *Tigress*. Reunited in Groton, the family settled down to make a new life on the periphery of the whaling community.

They were returning to a place they knew. With the Budingtons nearby and familiar whaling names lacing the area, it must have seemed not altogether unfamiliar; and yet, the setting was inland—far from a view of the sea. Not even tall masts were visible from Pleasant Valley. Ebierbing worked at becoming a farmer and carpenter. He continued fishing and hunting. His half brother, Italoo Enoch, visited from Cumberland Sound. Tookoolito got a sewing machine and made fur garments for sale. Groton resident Charles E. White remembered sitting on the floor in his house watching her chew furs to soften them before sewing. Punny went to school nearby at what was then called the North Lane, or Skunk Lane, or District No. 2 School—now the Pleasant Valley School. One of her playmates, Mary Walker Raymond of Hamden, wrote that Punny

> . . . *was not a bright pupil. Indeed it was with great difficulty that she learned anything at all. But she was a good little playmate, and with her broad, brown face, black, shining eyes, and very straight, black hair; with her little fur suit and cap with hanging tails, she makes a pleasant picture in my chamber of memories.*
>
> *Julia [her sister] and I, New Englanders for many generations, taught to conceal our feelings, could never quite understand the long, clinging kiss with which Hannah let her go from the gate in the morning, or the rapturous way in which she was caught up in her mother's arms at night, to receive many more kisses.*

Tookoolito, exhausted and sick with tuberculosis, clung to life as tight as she could. Ebierbing found that he could not adjust to a life of farming and decided to go back north, where he found employment with Captain Allen Young on the *Pandora*. Later, Ebierbing served on a vessel belonging to the U.S. Fish Commission.

Much of the time alone with Punny, Tookoolito continued on, igloo-wife of Groton. She shopped for groceries and necessities at the establishment of George L. Daboll. The Dabolls were a prominent Groton family intermarried with the Budingtons.

One of the curious documents to spill out from this period is an account book from the grocer. Inside, in ornate script, is a listing of her purchases, with their prices and the amount carried forward. Starting with March 27, 1874, and continuing through August 21, 1875, it holds probably one of the clearest records available of a semi-literate, foreign-born woman living as a single parent in rural America at the time: soda crackers, white meal, butter, pork, potatoes, turnips, oil, thread, sugar, tea, coffee, eggs, beef, rice, tobacco, soap, candles, camphor.

The list is more than a litany of commodities. It is also more than a snapshot of daily life at a particular time and place. It is a tracking of Tookoolito—of her needs, desires, and financial capabilities.

Among random papers is another small notebook in her writing, which appears to keep accounts. Only several pages are used. Starting with July 23, 1873 (soon after she had returned from Wiscasset to Groton): "old man give me 2 [?] dollars 43." Following, it appears that she got five dollars from Ebierbing on August 12. (Since he was off on the *Tigress*, this must indicate that she got some sort of payment from the Navy.) August 19, "Mr. Barley (or is it Bailey, her friend in Wiscasset?): 10 dollars." September 2, "three boxs, 2 dollars 22." There is figuring for boots and socks for Punna. The writing is difficult to read, the accounting in no particular form. A faintly sketched and wordless map follows, a final entry: Is this a doodling, an attempt to outline her new territory, or a poignant remembrance of coastlines left behind? Was she doing what so many Baffin Island women did—manifesting the terrain they carried inside themselves? In numerous instances, Hall had depended on their cartography.

Kafka said: "Writing is the axe that breaks the frozen sea within." But Tookoolito was not concerned with introspection. Like so many women of her time (1838–76), she was committed to the daily processes of maintenance and survival. It was not a period in which women were encouraged or enabled to reach beyond their domestic responsibilities. There were few opportunities and even fewer role models. Lady Jane Franklin (1791–1875), who moved governments, stands alone as a beacon of effective female energy.

Ironically, a woman gave her name to this period: Queen Victoria ascended the throne in 1837—the year before Tookoolito was born, and reigned for twenty-three years after Tookoolito's death. Although she was Britain's longest-ruling monarch and the empress of India, she was responsible more for setting moral tone than for ruling her country. That was done, while he lived, by her consort and cousin, Prince Albert, and otherwise by ministers and parliament. Tookoolito never forgot her meeting with Queen Victoria and Prince Albert, but aside from happy memories, not much came of the encounter. This, the Gilded Age, was a time when women and the poor did not fare well. The Queen was opposed to women's suffrage and to improving child labor laws. Modesty was given precedence over health and welfare.

It was also the time of Florence Nightingale—the "Lady with a Lamp"— the visionary who shed light on the execrable state of hospitals and reformed the nursing profession. On both sides of the Atlantic, women who were neither well known nor connected were beginning to organize as never before. The Industrial Revolution had brought them out of the home and into the workplace, but only to enter a new realm of exploitation. Now they began to demand fair treatment—suffrage, better pay, and improved working conditions. In the United States, the abolitionist movement and the temperance movement provided channels for political practice and pragmatism.

Yet, aside from the suffragists such as Elizabeth Cady Stanton and Susan B. Anthony, there were not many female voices heard or women recognized for their accomplishments during the lifetime of Tookoolito. In England, novelists George Eliot, the Brontë sisters, and Mary Shelley; in the United States, poet Emily Dickinson (whose work was published almost entirely after her death) and novelist Louisa May Alcott; astronomer Maria Mitchell, who was employed by the U.S. government; marine biologist Elizabeth Cary Agassiz, who became the first president of Radcliffe College; and actress Charlotte Cushman were among the exceptions.

In terms of physical endeavor and bravery, there are no relevant areas of comparison, with the possible exception of lighthouse keepers. In 1838, the year Tookoolito was born, a daring rescue of a foundered ship was made by William Darling, keeper of the Longstone Lighthouse in the Farne Islands. He was assisted by his twenty-three-year-old daughter Grace. Later reports exaggerated her role to the point where Grace Darling became a sentimental icon. A more real heroine of the rocks is Idawalley Zorada Lewis. Born in 1842, she inherited from her father title of Lighthouse Keeper at Lime Rock, Newport, Rhode Island. At age sixteen, she took over her disabled father's duties, and that year she rowed four shipwrecked men to safety. She is credited with saving the lives of fifteen during her forty-eight years at the post. She would have recognized, and appreciated, Tookoolito's accomplishments. But at a time when decorum counted more than courage, Tookoolito stood alone.

Because she did not attempt—nor probably desire in any way—to leave a written record, it is difficult to assemble a portrait from the pieces we have; and yet there are pieces enough to shape a tenuous outline—a penumbra.

The history of payment to Tookoolito and Ebierbing is difficult to parse and even more difficult to understand. When the couple first went to work for Hall, they were paid in kind—as were all Inuit in the whaling community of Cumberland Sound at the time. Food, guns, ammunition, knives, and wood were particularly desired by the local inhabitants. Tea kettles, trinkets, and clothes were also accepted currency. A native assistant who did particularly well might earn a whale boat—a payoff with tremendous bartering possibilities for the future. Ordinarily, a whaling captain would hand out daily or weekly food supplies to the families of the men in his "employment." This was largely coffee, tea, and ship's bread, or hard biscuits.

In his many small notebooks, Hall kept careful track of his disbursements. On March 15, 1869, for instance, he recorded the following: for the family of Ouela "while he is absent with me on our sledge journey to KWL [King William's Land]":

For wife	*Bread 11½ lbs.*
	Molasses 2 pints
+	
For his old mother	*Tobacco 2*
	Matches 2 Pks (100 in each)

On the left margin of his cramped note, he indicated that he was also giving one pound of coffee to each.

On a scrap of paper found among his correspondence to Captain Edward A. Chapel, he wrote: "Tobacco goes further with Innuits than anything else."

And so, inside the land of the Inuit people, the list of commodities is written over and over: Tobacco, bread, molasses, coffee, and matches were the currency. Outside, however, it was a matter of cash. In May 1864, when Hall was preparing to leave the United States on his second expedition, he listed a payment of five dollars to Tookoolito. During this month, he also listed, under "sundry expenses," "2 Esquimaux—3.59; meals for them for five days totaling 10.61; 1 pair shoes—3.80"; and then, a theft of $15 "from my pocket while riding in cars." He also spent fifty cents on medicine for Ebierbing and $8.00 on a trunk for Tookoolito. In September 1869, while packing up for the return trip home on the *Ansel Gibbs*, he lists "1 Seaman's chest (Hannah's)," while listing two trunks for "Joe."

While in the United States with Hall, Tookoolito and Ebierbing received irregular cash handouts, channeled through the largesse and organization of his backers, chief among them Henry Grinnell of New York and J.(James) Carson Brevoort of Brooklyn. Sometimes there were small presents from others. Sylvia Grinnell continued her kindness to the child named for her and corresponded with Tookoolito even after she had married and moved to England. As on the floe, much depended on the kindness of strangers. Hall made no provisions for regular or future support.

Once Tookoolito and Ebierbing came to Washington for the *Polaris* hearing in June 1873, they were able to establish something more of a presence with the Navy. There was an account set up to compensate them for the *Polaris* trip, and numerous drafts were made upon it. Occasional letters passed back and forth between Tookoolito and Hall's early champion, Colonel James Lupton of the U.S. Patent Office, regarding payments and their fine points (Joe's clothes on board the *Tigress* were not charged against the account but monthly payments of $20 to Tookoolito were). One disbursement, of $1,336, was given to Brevoort to pay off the mortgage on the house and lot.

Small sums and small purchases marked the time. On November 4, 1874, the day Lupton wrote to Tookoolito his letter explaining the payment for the mortgage, she bought twenty bars of soap for one dollar, twenty pounds of white meal for sixty cents, one sheet of wadding for five cents, and camphor for twenty-five cents. On average, Tookoolito went to the store every six days. Her most frequent purchase was soda crackers, which she would buy in quantities of two or three pounds at a time. On January 20, 1875, she bought two sticks of licorice for ten cents.

That was, perhaps, a last treat. On March 18, 1875, tragedy struck again. Punny was dead of tuberculosis or pneumonia. Her small, exhausted lungs had collapsed.

Some people remembered that she was buried first under a large pine tree in a corner of the family property, but her former playmate, Mary Walker Raymond, recalled: ". . . her body was laid at once in the grave in Starr cemetery, beside those of Cudilargo (sic) and Tukilikitar (sic)." The argument cannot be resolved.

Tookoolito had made a visit to Daboll's the day before Punny died, buying a gallon of molasses for eighty-five cents and a bottle of castor oil for nineteen cents. Did she hurry home from Daboll's to prepare a potion for her daughter? Even today, cold-pressed castor oil is used to alleviate a wide range of ailments, just as camphor, which she had bought earlier, is used to relieve congestion and to ease breathing. Was there a doctor? Did she have help that day and night, sitting up with her dying child? Did she remember, during her vigil, the death igloos and tupics of her native land and remember how Father Hall had insisted on staying with the dying in spite of everything she had been taught?

Three days after Punny's death, Tookoolito returned to Daboll's for six-and-a-quarter pounds of codfish and two balls of cotton yarn; six days after that for one pound white corn; and three days later for one plug tobacco and one stove handle. There is no way of knowing how the days stretched out for her or to know who, if any, stopped by the empty gate. Did Mary and Julia, on their way to or from school, take the time to greet their dead friend's mother? Did Sarah Budington come to visit? Were there letters of condolence? Notes and small gifts? Tea and vinegar, sugar, corn, calico, thread, and soda crackers: Somehow the days passed by, marked by purchases and pennies. The clerk at Daboll's, perhaps, got to look into her eyes once a week as she grew more tired, her breath more labored, or did she keep her eyes averted? Earth wobbled on its axis, and the once-unwavering North Star moved still farther away from the pole.

Somehow, Tookoolito, broken in health and spirit, continued to hold out after Punny's death. As Mary Walker Raymond commented, "Joe wanted Hannah to go back to the north with him; but she could not tear herself away from that little grave." Occasional letters found their way to her. She also received some checks from James Gordon Bennett, publisher of *The New York Herald*, who had purchased the *Pandora*, the vessel on which Ebierbing had been serving. Bennett, seeking for his paper a scoop as big as the discovery of the missing Dr. Livingstone in Africa, now refitted the *Pandora* as the *Jeannette* and prepared her for a try at the North Pole. Ebierbing received his final wages from Bennett in November 1875. He then signed on to a U.S. Fish Commission schooner and returned to Baffin Island. A few notes from the ship's company reached Tookoolito, informing her of Ebierbing's well-being, and one note included ten dollars. In a letter dated Washington, December 14, Hall's editor, Professor J. E. Nourse, asked John Copp to extend his sympathies to Tookoolito. We do not know if she received the message. On December 31, 1876, Tookoolito was dead at age thirty-eight.

There were those, including Nourse, who claimed that among her last words was the petition, "Come, Lord Jesus, and take thy poor creature home!" But these were her earnest Christian friends who wanted us to think well of her, and we do not know her last words. There were arguments as to whether she was buried first, alongside her two children on the family property, or immediately in the Starr Burying Ground. But there is no question about where she lies now. I went to see.

The Starr Burying Ground is found back of Route 12, off Pleasant Valley Road. If you come in off Route 12 by the Shell Station, you go down Pleasant Valley Road and past Pleasant Valley Elementary School. You turn right up Lestertown Road, and after a short drive, you come to the simple entrance to the Starr Burying Ground.

You turn right and keep to the right. This route takes you to the lower, older part of the cemetery, which began at Pleasant Valley Road and worked its way up the hill. There, by the road, I found stones dating back to 1759.

You come to a large oak tree and then you come to the obelisk of

Tookoolito's grave

Edmund and Betsey Ann Avery. Beyond this is the obelisk of Albert N. Ramsdell and his wife, Mary Jane Avery Ramsdell. In between these obelisks—surrounded by Averys—is the resting place of Tookoolito. It is a small and strangely crowded plot, about fifteen feet by fifteen feet, with three graves bearing strange names and words that are deeply weathered.

First, you see a tombstone relatively tall but not by comparison with its neighbors. Though the face is blotched with lichen, the inscription is easy to read. Under five ivy leaves appear the initials "J" and "H," followed in the next line by "Joseph Eberbing (sic)." Far below, appears "Hannah," and, in the following lines, "His wife/ Died Dec. 31, 1876/ Aged 38 years."

In front of Hannah's tomb stands a small stone for "Silvia (sic) Grinnell Ebierbing."

To the left of Punny's stone is one of similar size but different coloring. From top to bottom it reads: "Cudlargo (sic)/ died July 1, 1860./ aged 35 years; Tukilikitar [?]/ died Feb. 28, 1863./ aged 18 months; Oo See Cong/ died July 1, 1867./ aged 28 years."

This last stone, which has been broken in two, has been cemented together with a second stone for backing. The fault line breaks through Tukeliketa's name, making it illegible.

It is not just a question of legibility that makes it hard to understand who lies here. Both Kudlago and Oo See Cong died and were buried at sea. Ebierbing, who returned to the Arctic a final time in 1878 with Lieutenant Frederick Schwatka's expedition in search of Franklin relics, is not here, either.

Of the two smaller stones, Punny's is overall the more difficult to read. I came back to the graveyard with tracing paper and crayons, got down on my hands and knees, and attempted to do rubbings. It is almost too late even for these. I found:

Silvia Grinnell Ebierbing
(Punna)
Born at Igloolik, July, 1866
Died March 18, 1875
She was a survivor of the Polaris Expedition under Commander Charles Francis Hall, and was picked up with 19 (sic) others from an ice floe April 30, 1873, after a drift on the ice for a period of one hundred and ninety days and a distance of over twelve hundred miles.

I could not get the final piece. It seemed to be, "Of such is the kingdom of love." I wanted it to be "love," not "heaven." I wanted that very much. I wanted the long, clinging kiss at the gate. I did rubbing after rubbing, but the word—the final word—is nearly gone. I argued with myself but could not get it. I returned later in the day for another attempt but still could not resolve it.

Punny's story will soon be washed away by wind and rain, while Tookoolito's stays blank. The toddler Tukeliketa, whose name cannot be read, will remain bound together with absent strangers, while his father, Ebierbing, remains an enigma.

It is said that when Ebierbing came back to Groton and knelt to weed Tookoolito's grave, he exclaimed: "Hannah gone! Punna gone! Me go now again to King William's Land; if have to fight, me no care." That was when he made up his mind to go north again, never to return to the fields of Connecticut. He did go to King William's Land, successfully guiding Schwatka's expedition to discovery of Franklin remains and artifacts while setting new records for sledging. By the time the party set out from its winter camp on April 1, 1879, Ebierbing was remarried.

When you look past the graves, down the hill and over Pleasant Valley Road toward Route 12, you become more aware of the noise of traffic. Then, to the left, you see a large striped white and blue balloon anchored at a Mitsubishi dealer and, glinting through the trees, bright pieces of a fleet of cars.

Mercifully, all this is behind the graves. They face up the hill. Across the cemetery road on which you parked and eight generous rows up the hill, under a Christian cross, lie Sydney O. Budington (September 16, 1823–June 13, 1888) and his wife, Sarah H. Knowles Budington (July 29, 1821–August 7, 1889).

If you read the captain's biography in the genealogical compilation titled *The Budington/Buddington Family* by Richard Walter Nielson, you get the impression that the Inuit deceased were welcomed into the family plot:

> . . . *Strange names such as "Cud-la-go," "Too-koo-lito," "Punna Ebierbing" and "Tu-ke-li-keta" have their place of honor and remembrance beside the Captain and his family.* . . .

No. The Inuit dead are nowhere near the Captain. They are as separate in death as they were in life. And here, in the quiet space between, lie many of the secrets of the *Polaris*, its commander, its captain, its crew, and the impossible, conflicting dreams it carried north. Here lies the story that cannot die, the ancient tale of a man who would go north but for his enemies, a man whose death could not be avenged. If ever a burying ground were to be haunted, it is this—on a hillside in Groton far from the sight of the sea but firmly in its grip.

I returned to New London, got back on Amtrak, and traveled to New York. I reached my mother's about ten that Friday night. We had a pleasant chat and went to bed. The next morning she got up, then returned to bed, saying she felt tired and not well. That night, she began to retch and continued doing so through the next morning. At noon I took her to the emergency room at New York University Hospital on 33rd Street. Within a very short time, a young doctor was putting nitroglycerin pills under her tongue. My mother had had, or was having, myocardial infarction: a heart attack. An artery was blocked; not enough oxygen was getting to her heart. As pieces of the heart tissue died, cardiac enzymes began to enter her bloodstream, signaling the crisis and creating a graph to follow. She felt no pain, only nausea—not untypical, I learned, for an elderly person.

I stayed with my mother until about eight that night; she was still in the emergency room because there was no bed available in the cardiac unit. She was there the next day as well. All visitors were cleared out that afternoon for an hour when a female patient died. Soon after, I had to fly back to Seattle, bringing with me my nine-year-old granddaughter for a month's visit. I wondered if I would ever see my mother again.

She spent a month in the hospital but does not remember any of it—neither entering, leaving, nor a moment in between, though she remembers her bank card number and phone numbers. She remembers me. She returned home with seventeen medications and tanks of oxygen.

For some weeks later, when I talked to her on the phone or visited her, she coughed as if drowning; and she was. With her lungs at half capacity from emphysema and congestive heart failure causing her body to fill with water, she was foundering, and the island of her mind was almost swamped.

Now, she has a nurse with her all the time. She cannot be left alone. When she leaves her apartment, it is in a wheelchair. Remarkably, though— through careful manipulation of diuretics and other medications and through consistently attentive care—she has improved to the point where she no longer needs supplemental oxygen. She has come back from the edge.

I think of Tookoolito, who came to live and die alone in a little house a world away from home, a house that echoed with the Bible and not the shouts of the angakok. It was made of wood, not ice; it was square, not round; and still, she died alone, far from the bones and camps of her ancestors. I think of the long trail of mothers and grandmothers and how I take my place in that moving line.

We count out my mother's pills and confer often with her doctor: Can we increase the diuretic? What will be the effect on the other medications? How can we cover for vacationing nurses? We are having two armchairs in her apartment reupholstered, trying to replicate the chintz with a Chinese motif—a phoenix arising. But we have taken away most of her jewelry and valuables, except for her engagement ring and a heart-shaped diamond pin. We have sorted them and disposed of them. One lot has already gone to auction, the proceeds distributed. Her home has now become a more public place, and we are dependent on the kindness of strangers. Different nurses and their families and friends enter. We cannot monitor everyone who is in and out and do not want to regret later what might be missing. (When my mother's sister Virginia was dying a similar death—in this same place and bed—her ruby and diamond engagement ring disappeared.) We have disbursed some cash to lessen the tax burden. And there will be no operation to correct her blocked artery—no catheter or surgical interventions—no cardiopulmonary resuscitation, no mechanical respiration. We have signed, in multiple copies, the Health Care Proxy of New York State, papers of which she is unaware.

We shop for delicacies for my mother and spare no expense. Would she like raspberries, or strawberries, or poached salmon salad from Petak's? Are there white tulips—her favorites—for sale somewhere in the neighborhood? She coughs and coughs and cannot remember. She does not want to hear about heart trouble. She is very afraid of dying—or was. I think now the concept is hazy. There is very little of the past left; how can there be a future? The neurotransmitters—the bridges of memory—have fallen. From the center of the floe, you cannot tell what weather lies beyond.

The water is rising everywhere—at the North Pole, and especially around my mother's heart and inside her lungs. She has traveled a long way—eighty-five years—though she has barely left New York. Her piece of ice is almost gone. She has come to the edge of the angled land of doors and six-sided crystals—the world of snow, frost, sleet, rime, and flowers frozen across a winter's windowpane. When the water rises higher, and there is nothing else, she will join it—a swimmer in the ocean of miracles and gods.

Author's Note

T ookoolito, her husband Ebierbing, their family, friends, and acquaintances were Inuit who lived in the area stretching from Baffin Island in the east to Hudson Bay in the west in what is now known as Nunavut, Canada's newest province, established for governance by indigenous people on April 1, 1999. They spoke Inuktitut, originally an oral language with no written component. It is impossible to go back to the 1860s and the 1870s— the time of the story—and capture an exact and accurate rendering of the names as they were then spoken. In the nineteenth-century texts, we have versions given by foreigners (who were not linguists) as they heard them and wrote them down. Variations abound, and these are mixed with English monikers arbitrarily given. This is particularly true for place-names, which were continually evolving.

I have maintained the names as they appear in the principal source material—the writings of Charles Francis Hall. The only change I have made is to eliminate the hyphens he placed between each syllable. When there have been questions, particularly in regard to place-names, I have made use of the scholarship of Canadian historian W. Gillies Ross, an authority on arctic whaling and geography.

Tookoolito has been known by many names. Once, she signed a photograph of herself "Tookoolitoo," and that is how J. E. Nourse, who edited *Narrative of the Second Arctic Expedition Made by Charles F. Hall . . .* , spells her name. Margaret Penny, the whaling captain's wife who knew her, referred to her as "Tackritow." According to Ross, she was also referred to as Tackilictoo, Tickalictoo, Tickaluck-too, and Tarchuc-too; and today, on historic plaques, she is listed as Taqulittuq. The whalemen called her Hannah or Anne. Her husband, Ebierbing, Ross notes, was known as Hackboch, Harboch, Harkbah, and, today, as Ipirvik. Hall, and the whalers, called him Joe or Eskimo Joe.

A particularly significant place—the whaling harbor in Cumberland Sound where Tookoolito and Ebierbing start out on their adventures—is Kingmiksok. It is also Kimicksuic and Kimiksoke. Today it is Nimigen Island. Likewise, Niantilik, the harbor at the mouth of Cumberland Sound, is also Niatoolak, Niountelik, and Nyatlick, among other variations.

Similarly, there are inconsistencies in the spelling of American and European names. Captain Sydney O. Budington is often referred to as Buddington; members of his family appear to have chosen either version for themselves. Frederick Meyer is often Meyers, and Dr. Emil Bessels is often Bessel. One *Polaris* crew member is referred to alternately as Anthing and Aunting; another as Lindermann and Nindemann. In every case, I have chosen what I ascertained to be the correct version and maintained it. In quotations, the original spelling is kept.

The term "Inuit" is used throughout (the nineteenth-century spelling was "Innuit") instead of "Eskimo," except in original material, as quoted. Inuit means "the people" or "real people"; the singular of Inuit is "Inuk," or "person."

When it comes to the telling of arctic history, there are many questions of fact as well as spelling. It is not surprising when popular accounts go astray. Determining the "truth" can be as difficult as fixing position. The smudged historical record is blotted with gaps and contradictions. Set down in a time of rudimentary instruments and limited knowledge, often it was written with the mercurial ink of ego and in the tone of Christian proselytizing. And what there is of it is wearing away and not easily accessible. Fascination tugs. Why not fill in the empty places, put words in the mouths of the long dead, and claim the story for ourselves? For the simple reason that it is not ours.

In attempting to tell Tookoolito's story as accurately as possible, I have concentrated on the primary sources. These include the Charles Francis Hall

Collection at the Smithsonian Institution, the George E. Tyson papers at the National Archives and Records Administration, and the collection of papers and materials relating to Tookoolito and Ebierbing housed at the Indian & Colonial Research Center, Old Mystic, Connecticut. I have consulted the relevant secondary sources. Foremost of these is *Weird and Tragic Shores: The Story of Charles Francis Hall, Explorer* by Chauncey C. Loomis. I have set down only what can be found in the record. Flawed as that record might be, it is what stands. The evidence shimmers, luring us on, into the frozen wastes of illusion. It is tempting to follow, but, in honor of Tookoolito, I stop at the edge of the boundless.

Notes

Chapter One
How the Whales Led Tookoolito Away from Home

For background material on whaling, I have depended on *Arctic Whalers Icy Seas: Narratives of the Davis Strait Whale Fishery*, edited by W. Gillies Ross. Excerpts, in chronological order, cover the period from 1824 to the early 1900s and provide much detailed information on the process, history, and culture of whaling in and around Cumberland Sound. One chapter is devoted to the autobiography of George E. Tyson, including a short account of the *Polaris* expedition and its ice drift. Ross edited another essential source for this chapter: *This Distant and Unsurveyed Country: A Woman's Winter at Baffin Island, 1857–1858*. Carefully annotated, it is the journal of Margaret Penny, who accompanied her husband, Captain William Penny, on an overwintering whaling season in Cumberland Sound. As a longtime acquaintance of Tookoolito's, whom she had met previously in Britain, Mrs. Penny provides some significant glimpses into the life and setting of Tookoolito and provides certain details otherwise lost. Ross also provides in this exceptionally knowledgeable work information on the effects of the whaling industry on the local population and furnishes the numbers cited.

For more on Tookoolito's brother, Eenoolooapik, see Alexander McDonald's account of his trip to Aberdeen, Scotland, in *Arctic Whalers Icy Seas*, Chapter Seven. A short version of Eenoolooapik's story can be found in *Lobsticks and Stone Cairns: Human Landmarks in the Arctic*, edited by Richard C. Davis.

The critically needed map created by Eenoolooapik and William Penny became Admiralty chart 1255, "Davis Strait, Cumberland Isle," printed in 1840. For specific information on the history of names found in Cumberland Sound, see "Whaling-Era Toponymy of Cumberland Sound, Baffin Island" by Philip Goldring, *Canoma*, 1985. As the author points out, partly because the whalers depended on Inuit pilots such as Eenoolooapik, a number of the original Inuktitut names within Cumberland Sound survived, while others on Baffin Island were replaced.

When Tookoolito and Ebierbing traveled to England, they were accompanied by a seven-year-old boy not related to them. His name, according to Ross, was Hackaluckjoe (*This Distant and Unsurveyed Country*, p. 54). During the time Tookoolito, Ebierbing, and Hackaluckjoe were making their visit, Captain Penny brought to Aberdeen another Inuit youth, fourteen-year-old Neu Terrallie (ibid., p. 57). He may have returned to Cumberland Sound with the three other Inuit visitors on board Captain Penny's *Lady Franklin* and *Sophia* in the summer of 1855. In a rare, privately published book, *Eighteen Months on a Greenland Whaler*, by Joseph P. Faulkner (1878), we get a glimpse of what appears to be this young man, "Johnny Penny," who never got over his fascination with the horses and the watches he encountered in England. Faulkner presents a mocking description of what happened when "Johnny Penny" was presented with a watch sent from "friends in Britain retaining a lively interest in the little savage" (pp. 214–216 and 239–241).

All quotations from Charles Francis Hall in this chapter are from *Life with the Esquimaux*, published in 1864. This is the only book Hall succeeded in seeing through to publication and which, therefore, is truly reflective of his sentiments regarding Tookoolito, Ebierbing, their people, and their culture. It is a significant ethnographic study as well as one of historical importance: Hall, working through Tookoolito as interpreter, discovered much information regarding the Franklin expedition and the sixteenth-century explorations of Martin Frobisher. He collected and carefully annotated many artifacts from both predecessors. Although Franklin was his chief object, Hall succeeded in bringing to light and new attention the early entrepreneurial explorations of the Elizabethan adventurer Frobisher.

The definitive study of Charles Francis Hall is that by his biographer, Chauncey C. Loomis: *Weird and Tragic Shores: The Story of Charles Francis Hall, Explorer.*

For further information on religious beliefs and practices of the Cumberland Sound Inuit, see Franz Boas's *The Central Eskimo*, originally published in 1888. In this definitive work, Boas acknowledges the pioneering ethnography of Charles Francis Hall, who preceded him by twenty years. For further information, see Boas's later work, "The Eskimos of Baffin Land and Hudson Bay," *Bulletin of the American Museum of Natural History*, Vol. XV, Part I, 1901.

Knowing in advance how important his sledge would be, Hall had one constructed for his first trip based on the design of Elisha Kent Kane's favorite sledge, "Faith." It had runners thirteen feet long. He provides specifications in the appendix of his book (Vol. 2, p. 352).

Chapter Two
Track and Discoveries: Traveling with Hall

Information on Hall's second expedition is based on his journals located at the Smithsonian Institution and on the account published by the Navy: *Narrative of the Second Arctic Expedition Made by Charles F. Hall: His Voyage to Repulse Bay, Sledge Journeys to the Straits of Fury and Hecla and to King William's Land, and Residence among the Eskimos during the Years 1864–69*, edited by Professor J. E. Nourse of the United States Navy. Nourse was also a minister of the Presbyterian Church. Although his work in editing Hall's work is epic, he carefully chose what he—and the Navy—wanted known. For an accurate assessment, it is important to read Hall's personal statements.

The Nyack letters reveal some interesting details. Hall, Tookoolito, and Ebierbing lived, Tookoolito said to Mrs. Budington, high up on a mountain, where there were cool breezes and berries. Ebierbing would go into New York on errands for Mrs. Quick, with whom they lived, as well as for Hall and Hall's assistant, Captain Snow.

In commenting on the role of the angakok, Hall said: "The angeko's business is twofold: he ministers in behalf of the sick; and in behalf of the community in general. If a person falls ill the angeko is sent for. He comes, and, before proceeding to his peculiar work, demands payment for his services, stating his price, usually some article to which he has taken a liking. Whatever he demands must be given at once, otherwise the expected good result of the ministration would not follow." Once Hall was surprised to discover that Tookoolito had given Jennie, an angakok, an indispensable cooking pan and various garments in exchange for services rendered Ebierbing when he was ill. The angakok was willing to take on any practical problem or need. An unsuccessful *ankooting* was held in the hills at one point to try to get the pack ice out of the bay in order to free the *George Henry*. In rare instances, the command of the angakok was denied, especially in cases when wife-swapping was ordered.

Consistently, Hall proved himself incapable of working with white sailors whom he hired.

References to adoption, or the giving away of children, are not unusual. In *Frozen Ships: The Arctic Diary of Johann Miertsching, 1850–54*, the author tells the story of how Captain McClure offered a thick red shawl to a young woman. Saying she had nothing to give in return, she drew her baby from her hood and, "in great distress and still covering it with kisses," offered it in exchange. When told she could keep her baby, she expressed delight (p. 118).

Chapter Three
The Polaris *Bids Adieu to the Civilized World*

The story of the *Polaris* is based on the writings of George E. Tyson, from the original source material housed at the National Archives and Records Administration and from his book, *Arctic Experiences . . .* , edited by E. (Euphemia) Vale Blake and published in 1874. All quotations from Tyson are from his book. Exceptions, where noted, are from the original eight small field books written *in situ* with the one pencil Tyson had while on the ice. A secondary source is *Narrative of the North Polar Expedition. U.S. Ship Polaris, Captain Charles Francis Hall Commanding*, also produced by the Navy, edited by Rear Admiral C. H. Davis of the United States Navy. Because of

Davis's "failing health," final revisions and proofing for the last seven chapters were completed by J. E. Nourse.

Lady Jane Franklin was born December 4, 1791. When she visited Hall in the summer of 1870, she was seventy-eight years old. Traveling with her niece Sophia Cracroft, she had already made a stop in Sitka, Alaska, hoping that in the former capital of Russian America, previously known as New Archangel, she would find records misplaced in the transfer of the new territory to American control. (For more information on this episode, see *Lady Franklin Visits Sitka, Alaska, 1870: The Journal of Sophia Cracroft, Sir John Franklin's Niece*, edited by Robert N. DeArmond.) Lady Franklin would continue traveling and searching for information on her husband until her death on July 18, 1875, at age eighty-three.

The Congressional resolution for the voyage to the arctic regions was introduced in the House by Stevenson of Ohio and in the Senate by John Sherman of Ohio, brother of the general.

The story of the *Resolute*, a ship well known at the time, is a long one, which Gillies treats in *Arctic Whalers Icy Seas* (pp. 192–194). After restoration and return to England in 1856, she served until 1879. After her demolition, Queen Victoria had a desk made from some of her wood and presented it to President Rutherford B. Hayes, who placed it in the Oval Office of the White House.

The expeditions of Lieutenant Edwin de Haven of 1850, Dr. Elisha Kent Kane of 1853–55, and Dr. Isaac I. Hayes of 1860–61 were underwritten by Henry Grinnell.

Loomis's summation of the mysterious death of Hall is found on page 353 of *Weird and Tragic Shores*.

Chapter Four
Separation: The Drift Begins

Hall noted at length the difference in burial rites between white men and the inhabitants of Baffin Island. The remains of the latter were disposed of quickly. Depending on circumstances, the body was put in a shallow grave or simply covered with rocks or put on a ledge of rocks. At the head of the deceased were placed the utensils used during mortal life and, in the case of children, their toys. One of the most haunting views of an Inuit grave is given by Captain G. F. Lyon in *A Brief Narrative of an Unsuccessful Attempt to Reach Repulse Bay, through Sir Thomas Rowe's "Welcome," in His Majesty's Ship Griper, in the Year MDCCCXXIV.* He describes a child's grave, in which "A snow buntin[g] had found its way through the loose stones which composed this little tomb, and its now forsaken, neatly built nest, was found placed on the neck of the child" (p. 68). According to Boas (1888, p. 614), the grave is visited on the third day after the death and then a year later, as well as whenever relatives happen to be passing by it. During these visits, food is offered to the deceased. Hall gives a detailed account of these rituals in his description of a visit to the grave of Nukertou: "They took down small pieces of tuktoo [caribou] skin with the fur on, and of toodnoo [caribou fat]. When there, they stood around her grave, upon which they placed the articles they had brought. Then one of them stepped up, took a piece of the tuktoo, cut a slice and ate it, at the same time cutting off another slice and placing it under a stone by the grave. Then the knife was passed from one hand to the other, both hands being thrown behind the person. This form of shifting the implement was continued for perhaps a minute, the motions being accompanied by *constant talk with the dead.* Then a piece of tuktoo fur and some toodnoo were placed under the stone, with an exclamation signifying, 'Here, Nukertou, is something to eat and something to keep you warm.' Each of the Innuits also went through the same forms" (Vol. 2, p. 197).

Chapter Five
A Gift of Seals

According to Hall, when the lusty Ugarng reminisced about a trip he made to the United States in 1854–55 and a visit to New York, he remarked: "G— d—! Too much horse—too much house—too much white people. Women? Ah! Women great many—good!" (Vol. 1, p. 101).

July 20, 1869, Hall wrote: "Joe is quite equal to any of the Innuits of this country in his inclinations [desire for other women] this way. . . . Hannah, poor creature, had to accompany this terrible wife party [when Joe took two extra women along on a hunting trip] much against her will. If ever there was a woman that performed her duty faithfully, that woman is Hannah.

Without exception she treats Joe most kindly. . . . There is not a woman her equal in industry & skill that I have ever [encountered in] the Innuit race & yet Joe treats her as badly as he dare. He would treat her much worse if it were not for me. He delights in many women & with all my [?] I cannot restrain him from his <u>savage</u> course. . . ."

For treatment of the Sedna legend, see Boas (1888, pp. 583–591; and 1901, pp. 119–145). As Boas makes clear, practices and beliefs throughout Tookoolito's world were based on allegiance to the mother of sea mammals, the protecting deity.

William Scoresby Jr., was born in Yorkshire, England, in 1789, and named for his father, one of the best-known whaling captains of his day. At age ten, he accompanied his father on the first of a lifetime of voyages to the arctic fishing grounds. Later, he joined his father's ship, the *Resolution*, as apprentice and was on board at age sixteen when the ship reached 81°30', the highest latitude reached by any ship for some years. (Hall's record, with the *Polaris* in 1871, was 82°11'.) A student of chemistry, physics, and natural history, the younger Scoresby became a leading authority on matters related to the northern whale fishery. He died in 1857 after making a scientific voyage to Australia. His knowledgeable writings elicited enormous interest and helped whet the appetite for discovery of the Northwest Passage. It would not be until the work of Vermont photographer Wilson A. Bentley in the early part of the twentieth century that snowflakes would again receive such accurate depiction. Scoresby's comments on seals are found in Vol. 1, pages 508–517.

Tyson's words on his pet seal are surprisingly emotional: ". . . but one day I saw a young seal; it looked so pretty, with its pure white coat . . . and bright hazel eyes, that I took it up in my arms like a baby, and carried it along, talking and whistling to it by the way. The little creature looked at me, turning its head round to look up in my face without any apparent alarm, and seemingly soliciting me to give it something to eat. I thought I should take a great deal of comfort with my little pet . . . one of the men, with a malignancy impossible for me to understand, had pressed the life out of my only pet simply to gratify a brutal nature. Had I been quite sure who was the perpetrator, my indignation would have found other vent, I suspect, than words" (*Arctic Experiences*, pp. 89–90).

During a subsequent winter when Tyson was again in Cumberland

Sound, another whaler, Joseph Faulkner, noted the attempt on his ship to make a pet of a young seal, but this one escaped. Live seals were also captured for zoological gardens in England, where they soon died of starvation.

According to Boas, women were in charge of puppies, keeping them warm, feeding them regularly, and starting their early training by putting them into small harnesses—all on the ledge, or bed area, of the igloo, in front of the lamp, and tied to the wall by a trace (1888, p. 565). Hall stated: "The Innuits take as much care of their young dogs as they do of their children, and sometimes even more" (Vol. 2, p. 238).

Chapter Six
Ice: Drifting Down the Country in the Pack

Scoresby, who had traveled through 60,000 miles of the frozen sea, stated: "Of the inanimate productions of the Polar Seas, none perhaps excites so much interest and astonishment in a stranger, as the *ice* in its great abundance and variety" (Vol. 1, p. 225).

For the story of the *Diana*, see *From the Deep of the Sea: An Epic of the Arctic* by Charles Edward Smith, the surgeon on board. For the quotation from *The Edinburgh Scotsman*, see page 263. Dr. Smith's account, given in great detail, makes vivid the plight and the terror of being locked in the pack ice and provides an extraordinary story of heroism. As Ross points out, Smith took on a far greater role than that of surgeon: After the illness and death of the captain, he assumed leadership. He is credited with saving the ship and many of the crew.

For information on cannibalism in regard to the lost Franklin expedition, see *Frozen in Time: Unlocking the Secrets of the Franklin Expedition* by Owen Beattie and John Geiger. For accounts of cannibalism among the Inuit population, see Boas and the works of Knud Rasmussen and Peter Freuchen. Rasmussen's story of Ataguvtaluk is found in *Across Arctic America: Narrative of the Fifth Thule Expedition* (pp. 16–17). Freuchen's story can be found in *Arctic Adventure: My Life in the Frozen North* (p. 168). Both Rasmussen and Freuchen provide numerous other instances.

Chapter Seven
Light Returns; the Last Dog Dies

For the songs of Cumberland Sound, see Boas's "Texts from Cumberland Sound," *Bulletin of the American Museum of Natural History*, Vol. XV, Part I, 1901 (pp. 333–349). The one cited was collected in 1883.

Women could own dogs as well as men. In one journal entry, Hall notes a dog named Elephant that used to belong to Tookoolito. Tookoolito was also expert at driving the dogs as well as tracking for them.

When Barbekark singly brought down a caribou, it caused a great stir. So unusual was the accomplishment that many thought it was not possible, but the evidence proved it to be so: "As soon as the prize [the slain caribou] was on board, it was fairly distributed among the ship's company fore and aft, and my brave dog was greeted with many a word of praise for his remarkable hunting feat!" (Vol. 1, p. 239). A sibling of Barbekark's was known to be a particularly good seal dog.

Freuchen's comments on the sanitation role of dogs can be found in *The Peter Freuchen Reader* (pp. 50–51). Hall corroborates his statement with the following anecdote of what happened after Tookoolito cut his hair during his first trip out with her and Ebierbing: "I may here mention that, after this, when we vacated the snow-house, our dogs rushed in to devour whatever they could find, *digestible or not digestible*, and my locks were a portion of what they seized. In went my discarded hair to fill up their empty stomachs! A few days later, I saw the very same hirsute material, just as clipped from my head, lining a step leading to another igloo, having passed through the labyrinthian way from a dog's mouth onward" (Vol. 1, p. 210).

As wild as the dogs seemed, they were not wild animals, as Hall proved in an anecdote: In spite of taboos to the contrary, the mother of Nukerzhoo once captured a wolf cub and attempted to bring it up as a pet, hoping it would be a superior hunter for her. But when the young wolf was half grown, the dogs discovered their playmate was a different species—an enemy—and tore him to pieces (Nourse, pp. 239–240).

The names of dogs could be very important. Sometimes the angakok, to ward off disease, would change a sick person's name or consecrate him as a dog to Sedna. In the latter case, the person would get a dog's name and would have to wear a harness over his inner jacket for the rest of his life. Also, friends sometimes would exchange names, and dogs would be called by the names of friends as a token of regard.

The extraordinary statement regarding Budington that Tyson made in his field book is starred in pencil—whether by him or by someone else is impossible to tell. It does, however, stand out as the single most emotional and significant entry and certainly the most damning evidence against Budington of any relevant document.

Chapter Eight
Research: A Magnifying Glass to the Heart

Nukerzhoo's attempted rape of Tookoolito took place in January 1867 at Ship's Harbor, Repulse Bay, when she was alone in her igloo. She was saved by Patterson, a crew member from the *Ansel Gibbs*, who happened to pass by at the time.

Hans was haunted by his reputation. In Godhavn on September 10, 1873, Krarup Smith, Inspector of North-Greenland, wrote to Commander Braine of the *Juniata:* "I have been sorry to hear, that the Esquimo Hans Hendrick very nearly had deserted the 'Tigress' at Godhavn, before reaching Upernavik, because he on-board the 'Tigress' has been pursued by suspicions, and—as he used his wife [?]—even frequent threatening, which made his life on-board almost insupportable,—this arising from the unfounded accusations against him by Dr. Hayes concerning the death of Mr. Sonntag. Capt. Hall had made himself familiar with the particulars of this case, and did not believe in any guilt—proving this by taking with him Hans and his family" (Letter, National Archives and Records Administration, Washington, D.C., #45, M625, Roll 95).

A view of the entrance to Cumberland Sound—blocked by icebergs—is given by Dr. Robert Goodsir in his 1850 book, *An Arctic Voyage to Baffin's Bay and Lancaster Sound, in Search of Friends with Sir John Franklin* (p. 150). His brother Harry, also a doctor, disappeared with the Franklin expedition. Robert Goodsir's narrative is an account of the voyage of the *Advice*, which sailed under Captain William Penny to Lancaster Sound in 1849 in search of the missing expedition. Another description is given by Faulkner in his book: "We found it to be full of islands, barren, wild, and generally precipitous from the shore, with here and there bays scooped out in them, with narrow beach" (p. 83).

For a study of the Inuit spiritual views and the role of the *tornaq*, see Boas (1888, pp. 583–600; and 1901, pp. 119–162).

Chapter Nine
Polar Bears: The Power beyond Life

Examples of ship's doctors who were writers, other than Charles Edward Smith, are Alexander McDonald, Sir Robert Goodsir, and the unnamed surgeon of the Scottish whaler *Hercules*, whose journal is excerpted by Ross in *Arctic Whalers Icy Seas*. Elisha Kent Kane and Isaac I. Hayes were doctors who led expeditions and wrote of their experiences. Doctors might have tended to be good observers and writers but were not immune to the psychological pressures of the arctic winter. In *This Distant and Unsurveyed Country*, Ross gives the story of Dr. Robertson of the *Alibi* who went mad during the winter of 1856–57 in Cumberland Sound. He finally committed suicide by leaping overboard in July in the midst of a gale (pp. 46-47).

Coleridge's "The Destiny of Nations" was first written in 1796–97 and revised in 1816–34.

Polar bears, which Hall called the "lions of the north," are both clever and ferocious in their hunting. They have been known to attack boats and whales. According to Hall, they would kill walrus by hurling down rocks on them from cliffs overhead and seals by swimming beneath them and grabbing them from below.

Chapter Ten
End Things

Tookoolito's comments on the afterlife are found in Hall's appendix, Vol. 2, pages 317–318.

Along with other tales of cannibalism, Boas tells the story of Tookoolito's sister: "About 1820 another party left for Iglulik [Igloolik]. . . . When they returned, after an absence of three years, they praised the country . . . where they had spent some time . . . and by these tales, in 1835, induced three boat crews to leave Nettilling in order to visit this happy land. They were grievously disappointed and after many misfortunes they perished on the narrow isthmus of Ipiuting. Their bodies were found by the Iglulik Eskimo, who related that the poor fellows had resorted to cannibalism. Among those who perished was a sister of the famous Hannah (Taqulitu), the companion of Hall. . . ." (1888, p. 432). He also comments: "I do not know of any cases of famine arising from the absolute want of game, but only from the impossibility of reaching it. . . . Sometimes traveling parties that are not acquainted with the nature of the country which they visit are in want of food" (1888, p. 427).

An even larger disaster was averted in 1830 when nineteen vessels were lost and twelve damaged in Melville Bay, but with no loss of life. Nearly a thousand shipwrecked mariners even managed to make merry in tent cities on the ice. Goodsir tells the extraordinary episode of "Baffin Fair" (pp. 46–48). Freuchen's story of the Saunders Island rescue is found in "Melville Bay and the Whalers," *The Peter Freuchen Reader* (p. 85). Hall's account of the rescue of the abandoned child Etu appears in Vol. 2, page 39. Strangely, Etu, whose father considered him a monster, was marked like a seal, with white and black spots.

Chapter Eleven
The Navy Inquiry: Letting Loose the Ghost

The principal source for the story of the *Polaris* after the Separation is *Narrative of the North Polar Expedition* . . . edited by Rear Admiral C. H. Davis. Like Nourse's *Narrative of the Second Arctic Expedition* . . . , it weighs five pounds; it is detailed and appears comprehensive but is flawed by its bias. As Loomis says of this work: ". . . Davis gave the impression that the expedition had been a Boy Scout Jamboree—a bit rough, of course, but enlivened by good cheer and boyish high jinks. The original source materials that Davis had used and distorted show how false that impression was" (p. 338).

Tyson's concerns about the population of Cumberland Sound are borne out by the comments of Ross in *This Distant and Unsurveyed Country.* When Captain and Mrs. Penny arrived at Niantilik in August 1857, they found four women, two babies, and a blind man, all starving and sick, who had been abandoned by the men who had gone off with a whaler instead of attending to the hunting needs of their people (p. 113). As the hunting cycles broke down, the people of Cumberland Sound became increasingly dependent on the handouts of the whalers, and hunger was exacerbated by disease and the added burden of half-white children.

What Tyson's editor, Euphemia Vale Blake, had to say of the hearing was: "After what had happened, the country would scarcely have been surprised had the buried commander arisen from his frozen grave and haunted some of the fugitives on their flight through the Arctic zone, across the Atlantic waves, to finally confront them in the very place and in the very presence where his great hopes had been so nobly helped and cherished" (pp. 406–407).

Chapter Twelve
Groton: The Final Years

The comments of Mary Walker Raymond of Hamden and of Charles E. White of Groton are found in *The New London Day,* June 3, 1939.

All letters referred to and quoted from are housed at the Indian & Colonial Research Center, Old Mystic, Connecticut.

Originally, Tookoolito had three account books from Daboll's, but only one remains.

Colonel James Lupton, originally from Hall's hometown of Cincinnati, was one of the explorer's earliest backers and one of the first for whom Hall named a geographical point, a channel in Frobisher Bay in 1861. In 1871, he affixed his name to the cape forming the north arm of Polaris Bay. It was Lupton who introduced Hall to Senator Sherman and Representative Stevenson of Ohio, who went on to push through Congress a bill in support of a North Pole expedition. He appears with Hall in the one recognized photograph of the explorer, taken in Washington in the winter of 1870.

Nourse provides the text of Punny's epitaph. The final, now illegible, word is "heaven."

A listing of Starr Burying Ground headstone inscriptions compiled in 1932 as a government project of the Great Depression further confuses the issue. Punny, for instance, is listed as "Inmuts, Silvia G. E., adopted daughter of Joe & Hannah. . . ." The list can be found in the Groton, Connecticut, Public Library.

Bibliography

Unpublished Material

Charles Francis Hall Collection: National Museum of American History, Smithsonian Institution, Washington, D.C.

George E. Tyson Collection: National Archives and Records Administration, College Park, Maryland

Letters and manuscripts related to Tookoolito, Ebierbing, Punny, the Budingtons, and Charles Francis Hall: The Indian & Colonial Research Center, Old Mystic, Connecticut

Published Material

By Charles Francis Hall:

Life with the Esquimaux: The Narrative of Captain Charles Francis Hall of the Whaling Barque "George Henry," from the 29th May, 1860, to the 13th September, 1862 . . . (London: Sampson Low, Son, and Marston, 1864).

Edited from the notes and journals of Charles Francis Hall:

Narrative of the Second Arctic Expedition Made by Charles F. Hall, 1864–69 . . . , edited by J. E. Nourse. (Washington, D.C.: Government Printing Office, 1879).

Edited from the notes and letters of Charles Francis Hall and others:

Narrative of the North Polar Expedition: U.S. Ship Polaris, edited by C. H. Davis (Washington, D.C.: Government Printing Office, 1876).

U.S. Navy Report on the *Polaris*:

Report to the President of the United States of the Action of the Navy Department in the Matter of the Disaster to the United States Exploring Expedition toward the North Pole: Accompanied by a Report of the Examination of the Rescued Party, etc., by the United States Navy Department (Washington, D.C.: Government Printing Office, 1873).

Biography of Charles Francis Hall:

Weird and Tragic Shores: The Story of Charles Francis Hall, Explorer, by Chauncey C. Loomis (New York: Alfred A. Knopf, 1971; University of Nebraska Press, 1991; New American Library, 2000).

Principal Source for the Ice Floe Drift:

Arctic Experiences: Containing Capt. George E. Tyson's Wonderful Drift on the Ice-Floe, A History of the Polaris Expedition, the Cruise of the Tigress, and Rescue of the Polaris Survivors, edited by E. Vale Blake (New York: Harper & Brothers, Publishers, 1874).

Contemporary (Post-1900) Sources

Beattie, Owen, and John Geiger. *Frozen in Time: Unlocking the Secrets of the Franklin Expedition* (Vancouver; New York: Greystone Books, 1998).

Bentley, W. A., and W. J. Humphreys. *Snow Crystals* (New York: Dover, 1962).

Berton, Pierre. *The Arctic Grail: The Quest for the North West Passage and the North Pole, 1818–1909.* (New York: Viking Penguin, 1988).

Bierhorst, John, ed. *The Dancing Fox: Arctic Folktales* (New York: Morrow, 1997).

Birket-Smith, Kaj. *The Eskimos.* Foreword by C. Daryll Forde. Translated from the Danish by W. E. Calvert. (London: Methuen, 1959).

Bonner, W. Nigel. *Seals and Sea Lions of the World* (New York: Facts on File, 1994).

Burgess, Helen. "Tookoolito of Cumberland Sound," *North*, Vol. XV, Number 1: January-February 1968.

Crouse, Nellis M. *The Search for the North Pole* (New York: Richard R. Smith, 1947).

Davis, Richard C., ed. *Lobsticks and Stone Cairns: Human Landmarks in the Arctic* (Calgary: University of Calgary Press, 1996).

Druett, Joan. *She Captains: Heroines and Hellions of the Sea* (New York: Simon & Schuster, 2000).

Eber, Dorothy Harley. *When the Whalers Were up North: Inuit Memories from the Eastern Arctic* (Norman, Oklahoma: University of Oklahoma Press, 1996).

Evans, Sara M. *Born for Liberty: A History of Women in America* (New York: The Free Press, 1989).

Farre, Rowena. *Seal Morning* (New York: Rinehart & Co., Inc., 1957).

Freuchen, Peter. *Arctic Adventure: My Life in the Frozen North* (New York: Farrar & Rinehart, Inc., 1935).

———. *The Peter Freuchen Reader* (New York: J. Messner, 1965).

Goldring, Philip. "Whaling-Era Toponymy of Cumberland Sound, Baffin Island," *Canoma*, 1985, pages 28–34.

Harper, Kenn. *Give Me My Father's Body: The Life of Minik, the New York Eskimo* (South Royalton, Vermont: Steerforth Press, 2000).

Jones, A. G. E., ed. *Polar Portraits: Collected Papers* (Caedmon of Whitby, 1992).

Kimball, Carol W. "Hannah, a Tiny Eskimo Woman," *Groton Standard*, July 8, 1982.

———. "Hannah: Groton's Lady Eskimo," *Tidings*, June 1991.

Macdonald, Fiona. *Women in 19th-Century America* (New York: Peter Bedrick Books, 1999).

MacDonald, John. *The Arctic Sky: Inuit Astronomy, Star Lore, and Legend* (Royal Ontario Museum/Nunavut Research Institute, 1998).

Macksey, Joan, and Kenneth Macksey. *The Book of Women's Achievements* (New York: Stein and Day, 1976).

Mangelsen, Thomas D., and Fred Bruemmer. *Polar Dance: Born of the North Wind* (Omaha, Nebraska: Images of Nature, 1997).

Maxwell, Gavin. *Seals of the World* (Boston: Houghton Mifflin Co., 1967).

Mowat, Farley. *The Polar Passion: The Quest for the North Pole* (Boston: Atlantic-Little, Brown, 1967).

Newsweek, "The Mercury's Rising," December 4, 2000.

Nielson, Richard Walter. *The Budington/Buddington Family* (Westport, Connecticut: Nielson Publishing Co., 1989).

Norman, Howard A., ed. *The Girl Who Dreamed Only Geese, and Other Tales of the Far North* (New York: Harcourt Brace, 1997).

Praded, Joni. "The Heat Is On: Hudson Bay Polar Bears Sweat Out Global Warming," *Animals*, July/August 2000.

Rasky, Frank. *The Polar Voyagers: Explorers of the North* (Toronto; New York: McGraw-Hill Ryerson, Ltd., 1976).